MAN IN THE MIDDLE

MAN IN
THE MIDDLE

A Story of the Polish Resistance:
1940–45

WITOLD SAGAJLLO

Leo Cooper in Association with
Secker & Warburg

First published in Great Britain in 1984 by Leo Cooper
in association with Martin Secker & Warburg Ltd,
54 Poland Street, London W1V 3DF

ISBN 0-436-44079-2

Photoset by Wyvern Typesetting Ltd, Bristol
Printed in Great Britain by Biddles Ltd,
Guildford and King's Lynn

To all those
who fought with me
I dedicate this book.

.

Contents

Acknowledgements

I should like to express my deepest gratitude to my wife Irena for her unstinting support; also to my son Andrew, without whose encouragement I would not have written this book and without whose perseverance this project would not have come to fruition.

List of Illustrations

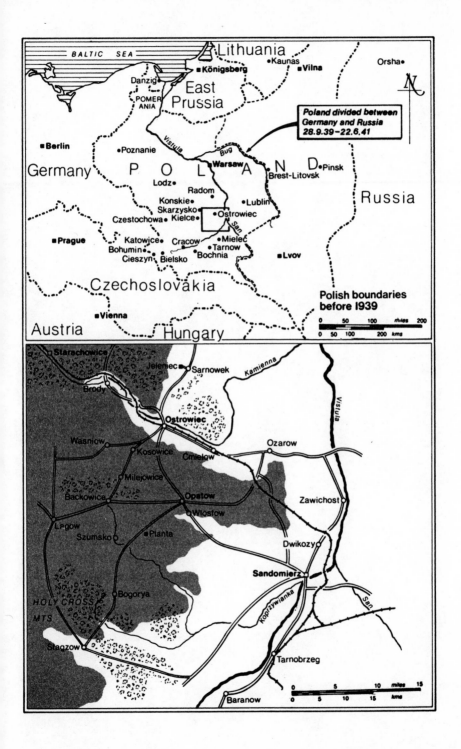

BALTIC SEA

Lithuania

Orsha•

•Königsberg

•Kaunas   •Vilna

Danzig

POMER-
ANIA

**East
Prussia**

•Berlin

**Poland divided between
Germany and Russia
28.9.39–22.6.41**

•Poznanie

Vistula

Bug

Warsaw

P   O   L

A   N   D•Pinsk

Germany

Lodz•

Brest-Litovsk•

Russia

Radom•

Konske•   •Lublin

Skarzysko•

Czestochowa• Kielce• •Ostrowiec

•Prague

Katowjce• Cracow• •Mielec

San

Bohumin•   •Tarnow

Cieszyn• Bielsko• Bochnia•

•Lvov

Czechoslovakia

**Polish boundaries
before 1939**

| 0 | 50 | 100 | rhiles | 200 |
| 0 | 50 | 100 | 200 | kms |

•Vienna

Austria   **Hungary**

•Starachowice

Jelemec •Sarnowek

Kamienna

Brody

Vistula

Ostrowiec

Wasniow

Ozarow

•Kosowice Cmielow

•Milejowice

Zawichost

Backowice

Opatow

•Wlostow

Lpgow

Szumsko   •Planta

Dwikozy

Sandomierz

Koprzywianka

San

**HOLY CROSS
MTS**

•Bogorya

Stagzow

Tarnobrzeg

| 0 | 5 | 10 | miles | 15 |
| 0 | 5 | 10 | 15 | kms |

Baranow

Foreword

Of all the historic nations of Europe the one whose very existence has been the most precarious during the past few hundred years is Poland. Her boundaries have frequently been changed, with and without her agreement, and her people have constantly been aware of the threat from larger and more powerful neighbours. Her geographical position on the wide spaces of the North European Plain has not been conducive to secure frontiers and her fear of the Germans to the West and Russians to the East has on several occasions proved justified. It was indeed Prussia, Austria and Russia who participated in the three partitions of Poland in the late eighteenth century, reducing Poland from a sizeable nation to non-existence in the space of a few years. Her re-creation following the First World War was achieved without any real guarantee of her boundaries. She now faced an emergent Soviet Union on one side and a united, albeit unarmed, Germany on the other. The increasing strength, politically and militarily, of the Soviet Union and the rearming of Germany under Hitler led Poland to believe that, after only twenty years of independence, she might again be crushed between powerful neighbours. The expected demand by Hitler for a return of Danzig and the Polish corridor to Germany, following quickly upon the occupation of Prague, was the portent of invasion. The defensive treaty rapidly signed by Britain and France with Poland was not enough to save her, and the Soviet-German non-aggression pact was the spark which lit the conflagration. Free from fear of a war on two fronts, Germany was able to prepare for invasion and on 1 September, 1939, forty-five German divisions, supported by 1,500 aircraft, launched their attack. Two weeks later the Soviet Union occupied eastern Poland under the terms of the Nazi-Soviet Pact. In a few weeks the fourth partition of Poland was complete, the Polish state had ceased to exist and many members of its government were in exile.

But what of her people? In a situation like this, when a country has been occupied, its citizens have few alternatives. Emigration is one, but for those who choose to remain the options are limited. Basically the choice lies between active co-operation with the occupying forces, acquiescence while awaiting liberation, and active opposition. Within all countries there are citizens who will make each of these choices, and in the occupied countries of Europe this was indeed the case. For those of us who live in countries which have not been occupied for hundreds of years, it is possibly difficult to realize the nature of occupation, yet many of us believe that we would resist the unwelcome invasion of our country. This is much easier said than done. The decision actively to oppose an occupying force is a courageous one, as many people in the occupied countries of Europe during the Second World War found to their cost.

This book is about a man who had to make such a decision, a man who chose to resist. Witold Sagajllo, known to his friends as Vic, was born near Orsha in what is now the Soviet Union, although it had once been part of Poland. As an educated Pole and an officer in the Polish navy, Vic recognized only too well the ominous political and military activity in Hitler's Germany in the 1930s and the growing might of the Soviet Union. When the invasion came and the gallant Polish resistance was overcome, first by the Germans in the west and then by the Soviet Union in the east of Poland, Vic resolved to escape to Britain and join the Polish forces in exile. Thwarted in his early efforts to achieve this, he remained in German-occupied Poland in order to lead a resistance group in the countryside. The concentration and labour camps of Poland and the Katyn and other massacres bear witness to what happened to educated Polish officers if they were caught by either the Germans or the Russians.

A man of deeply-held convictions, an avowed anti-fascist and anti-communist, fighting for the freedom and independence of his country, the extraordinary exploits of Witold Sagajllo are set out in this book. The arrival of the Soviet 'liberation' forces was not seen by Vic, or many other Poles, as the freedom for which they had been fighting and caused many, whose anti-communist views were known, to seek exile. Displaying the tenacity which had helped him survive during the German occupation, Vic was able to escape with his family across Europe to Italy, and eventually to Britain. It is in Britain that Vic and his family have found the freedom and peace which they desperately sought for Poland.

My own encounters with Vic began at the bridge table in the college where we both lectured some fourteen years ago. His keen mind and sharp wit are as evident at the bridge and chess table today as they must have been to enable him to survive in the forests and fields of Poland. Vic is unlikely to see those forests and fields again, though he and his wife, Irene, still watch events in Poland with as much concern and passion as when they were in their homeland. In the same way that they found unreal the expectation that the Soviet Union, despite its occupation of eastern Poland in 1939, would become an ally and a friend following the German invasion of 1941, so they regard the present 'friendship' between Poland and the Soviet Union as unreal. The physical struggle for Vic might be over, but the mental anguish and emotional pain remain as evidence of a man's love for his country and for freedom. This book is a testimony to that freedom, to a freedom which we all too easily take for granted, and at the same time it is a reminder of the continuing struggle against tyranny and occupation in many parts of the world.

BRIAN L CHALKLEY
Lecturer in European Studies
College of Technology
Taunton
1984

Preface

Many books have been written about the Underground Movements in Europe during the Second World War. Very few have been written about the Underground in Poland, and those there are were written either without first-hand knowledge of the conditions then prevailing, or at the instigation of the present Warsaw Government and so give a completely false picture of the part played by the Communists.

Throughout her history Poland has had to fight on two fronts: Tartars, Turks and eventually Russians in the East; and the *Drang nach Osten* in the West. She lost her independence in 1795 when she was partitioned between Prussia, Russia and Austria. She regained it in 1919, after the First World War, and twenty years later, in 1939, she lost it again. Attacked from the West by Germany on 1 September, 1939, she finally succumbed when invaded from the East on 17 September by Soviet Russia. Poland was again divided, this time into two parts. The German-occupied territory was West of the old Curzon Line. Silesia, Pomerania and Posnan were incorporated into the Third Reich. The rest became the so-called General Gouvernement under Governor-General Frank.

Very soon the patterns of behaviour of the occupying powers were established: in the Russian Zone mass arrests and deportations; in the German Zone the introduction of starvation rationing, the segregation of Jews, the arrest of all prominent public figures not yet in hiding, deportation for slave labour, summary mass executions for any act of sabotage —all in the name of Teutonic law and order.

By the end of September, 1939, after the collapse of the defence of Warsaw, the Underground Resistance Movement had already been established. People from all strata of society came together to provide false identity documents, to establish escape routes to Hungary and hence to the West, to counteract terror with terror. The Communists, very few in numbers, sat tight, not committing themselves. After all, their Russian comrades were in alliance with the Germans.

After 21 June, 1941 when the Germans attacked Russia, the situation of the Polish underground authorities, military and civil, became very difficult. It became, one might say, unique among the subjugated nations of Europe. They had to oppose the recognized enemy, Germany, and at the same time had to find some sort of *modus vivendi* with the other unofficial, but perhaps more deadly enemy, Russia, now officially an ally.

This was the situation with which this book deals. It is not a personal account of the author's life or of the life of his family. Where he, his wife or his son appear, they are mentioned only in so far as they are pertinent to the situation in occupied Poland and to the chaos in Europe just after the war. It is not about heroics, but gives a *true* picture, gained at first hand, of underground life and of the associated problems faced by the Poles during the German occupation of their country. It describes the problems of containing the German terror with as few Polish losses as possible, and the new terror introduced by the Communists. It tells of one man's efforts to survive both the German occupation and the so-called Russian 'liberation', and how he managed, together with his wife and son, to escape to the West after the end of the war in Europe.

It is intended to be of interest to all who have only the vaguest idea about the methods by which the Russians obtain power. It gives some insight into Russian psychology, and into our psychology as seen by the Russians. It should also be of interest to any man or woman who loves freedom as we know it in the West.

It is a topical book because, since the end of the Second World War the Russians have used the same methods in all countries which have become their satellites or have fallen into the orbit of their interests: East Germany, Poland, Czechoslovakia, Bulgaria, Romania, Estonia, Latvia, Lithuania, Vietnam, Cuba, Angola, South Yemen, Ethiopia and last, but not least, Afghanistan. The Russians will use the same methods whenever, and wherever, they are allowed to do so, either through military weakness or political negligence.

All the characters in the book are real. Some have been murdered by the Security Forces (either Polish or Russian—there is no difference); some died in prison; some escaped to the West. The majority stayed behind. It is because of those who stayed behind that pseudonyms have been used. Whether they can be 'deciphered' by the Security Forces or not is difficult to say; one never knows with the Communists.

The book is dedicated to the memory of those who died, and to all who are still alive, there or here. All share the same knowledge and the same feelings: that their efforts to regain their freedom have been shown to be completely futile.

W. S.

I

The Russian Menace

IN ORDER FULLY to understand the predicament in which the Polish nation found itself during and after the Second World War, one has to look, even if only cursorily, at Russia, and its relationship with Poland over the last three hundred years. The history of Russia provides a peephole into what they themselves like to call 'the Russian soul'. For nearly four hundred years Russia, or, as it then was, the Duchy of Moscow, a country to the east of the River Dnieper, was under the domination of the Tartars. In the tenth century it was converted to Christianity. The Tartar domination was ended by Tsar Ivan III (1462–1505). His successor, Ivan the Terrible (1533–84), began to consolidate the Tsar's power. He established the 'Oprichina', the ancestor of the Tsarist Ochrana, the Bolshevik Cheka, GPU, NKVD and now the KGB.

Ivan the Terrible cast an envious look at his western frontiers and instigated a series of wars against Poland, wars which continued on and off until the first partition of the country in 1792. On the whole the Poles had the upper hand in these wars. In 1610 the Polish King Wladyslaw (Ladislaus) IV Vasa was actually elected Tsar of Moscow. Unfortunately, the condition of taking the throne was that he had to be crowned in the Russian Orthodox cathedral in Moscow. The Pope vetoed this idea. The King, therefore, could not accept the offer and Rome thus changed the future of Europe.

1

The eighteenth century saw the beginning of the disintegration of the Polish state (known then simply as Rzeczpospolita (Res Publica). Russia, Prussia and Austria took full advantage of the weakness of the Poles and the first partition of the Res Publica followed in 1792. In 1793 Russia forced the second partition. An insurrection led by Kosciuszko was ferociously suppressed and the third partition took place in 1795.

The next sixty years saw several Polish uprisings: the insurrection against Russia of November, 1830–31; the Cracow insurrection against Austria in 1846, the year of the Spring of the Nations; the Poznan insurrection against Prussia in 1848; and finally, the last and the greatest of all, the January insurrection of 1863 against Russia. All were followed by mass arrests and convictions. The Russian response was always the most brutal. Inevitably it included mass hangings and deportations to Siberia.

It was during this period of Polish history that the terms 'Poland' and 'Polish' actually came into general usage, as the antithesis to Russia, Prussia or Austria, to Russian, German or Austrian.

It is difficult to analyse the historical process by which the Russian character, the 'Russian soul' has been shaped. The Tartar domination, the incursions of the Norsemen, Christianity from Byzantium, all contributed to this 'soul', each influence opposing the others. It has been described by an anonymous writer in 1947 as 'mysterious, disturbing, exotic, oscillating all the time between holiness and crime, always looking for something new and not being able to live in the real world; longing for God and willingly submitting itself to the Devil; helpless in the Good and horrible and revelling in the Evil; persecuted by its own rulers and pitiless in the persecution of others; rebelling against oppression, and subjugating millions of alien nations; prone to religious mysticism and at the same time Asiatically sly and cunning; certain of its mission and suffering at the same time from an inferiority complex in the face of Western culture; shameless to the extreme and at the same time distrustful and reticent.' It was shaped on the one hand by the Christian culture of Byzantium modified by the individualism of ancient Greece and on the other by the characteristics of the nomadic Tartar hordes, blindly obeying the whims of their despotic rulers. The influence of Western culture and technology, introduced by Peter the Great, was very superficial, affecting the ruling classes only, leaving the bulk of the nation unchanged, totally removed from the social and political ideology of the rest of Europe.

Although seemingly poles apart, there was in fact a tight ideological bond between the Russian rulers and the masses they ruled. This bond made it possible for Russian governments to develop imperialistic tendencies in the masses themselves. By simply replacing the absolutist régime of the Tsarist governments by the tyrannical régime of the Bolsheviks, the Great Revolution of 1917 did not in effect change anything in the life of the Russian nation. Moreover, all who were tainted to any extent by Western culture and civilization either escaped to the West or were liquidated. In Tsarist Russia, while the administration was corrupt, the judiciary was less so. As a result, the law was on the whole enforced, according to the statutes. The statutes themselves were quite arbitrarily imposed by the simple expedient of publishing the Tsar's decrees, known as 'Ukazy'. Whether or not they were just or reasonable is another matter. Jews, for instance, had no right to settle east of an arbitrary demarcation line. Poles had no right to buy land to the east of another arbitrary demarcation line. The Socialist Party was banned. The teaching language in the State schools had to be Russian. Other examples are too numerous to mention. But the individual accused of breaking the law, which, in each case, was quite explicit, had the right to a defence counsel, and his or her guilt had to be proved beyond doubt by the prosecution. If proof was lacking or inadequate the accused was discharged. With the advent of the USSR, the judicial process, in our Western sense of the word, ceased to exist. Every subsequent trial has become a farce.

The imposition on the political and social life of Russia of the theories of Marx and Engels, albeit modified, made it possible to abjure the complexities of Western political life, though its theorists themselves were Western. Total rejection of the Christian ethic legitimized the imposition of an absolute system of government. The Iron Curtain was in position long before Churchill's Fulton speech.

That was the country and the culture which the newly reborn Poland had to face in 1919.

In 1919 Marshal Pilsudski, then the leader of the Polish nation, tried to weaken once and for all the strength of Soviet Russia. He set out to help the Ukrainians in their effort to gain independence. The Polish army moved to the East, reached the River Dnieper and for a short time occupied Kiev. His attempt failed. The Poles were forced to retreat under the pressure of overwhelming Russian superiority in manpower. The issue was eventually settled by the Battle of Warsaw in August, 1920, at which the Red Army was heavily defeated and a peace treaty was signed with the Soviet régime at Riga in 1921.

I believe that the Soviets have neither forgotten nor forgiven the defeat, or the peace treaty itself. The frontier with Soviet Russia was always sensitive. The Communist Party in Poland was banned. Polish plans for general mobilization were drawn up on the assumption that the attack would come from the East, from Poland's perennial enemy.

I have mentioned that even the pre-Revolutionary Russians suffered from an inferiority complex. I believe that the intensity of this complex increased after the Revolution. Carl Jung regards a neurosis not simply as a negative disorder but as a disorder contributing to the formation of personality. Soviet Communism introduced into the life of the nation, among other ideas, hatred—hatred of Christianity; hatred of every Western concept of life, individual or collective.

4

As a Christian I believe that part of the Jung's collective and individual unconscious, of the archetype, of one of the *Ideae Principales* of St Augustine, tells us that hatred is a negative feeling. When the conscious begins to hate, there is conflict between conscious and unconscious, resulting in neurosis: the inferiority complex.

As a child during the Great Revolution I could observe and experience the manifestation of hatred in Bolshevik behaviour. As an adult I could see and feel it in the actions and the behaviour of Communists both during the German Occupation and afterwards. All through history Poland has represented the West, a fact which the Russian people have never accepted, or even understood. Hence their hatred and their fear. This attitude is what the Polish nation had to cope with in 1939, to suffer throughout the war and afterwards and has to deal with now.

II

Six White Ducks

EARŁY IN MAY 1941 I left Radom, a town about sixty miles south of Warsaw, on the 7 am train to Cracow. At Skarzysko, a railway junction thirty miles south of Radom and midway between Radom and Kielce, capital of the province of that name, I changed to the train running east to Lublin, a university town east of the Vistula.

I boarded the last coach, a fourth-class coach, a few of which were still in operation on railways of the General Gouvernement (the name given to that part of Poland occupied by the Germans after the 1939 débâcle but not incorporated into the Third Reich). The coach had no compartments, only a few benches around the sides and an empty space in the middle.

I looked around carefully. The passengers consisted of a dozen women, a nondescript man of about thirty, with a well-worn face, a black stubble of beard and deep wrinkles round his eyes, and a young man who kept himself well apart from the others, an elegant young man with chamois-leather gloves, a Borsalino hat and an elegant summer overcoat buttoned at the top and at the bottom, with the two middle buttons left undone. A beautiful pig-skin suitcase was at his feet. He seemed quite calm and unconcerned with what was going on around him. I could see, all the same, that his eyes were watchful, sizing me up along with the others, watching every move, listening to every word spoken by the women passengers.

The women were surrounded by baskets, bundles and sacks, some full, some apparently empty. Smugglers, I thought.

The smuggling of food was essential for survival in occupied Poland. It was organized on an ad hoc basis. Somebody, somewhere, would have a cousin or a friend who had slaughtered a pig, or had hidden some extra grain, or had managed to produce a few kilos of butter. The family, friends and neighbours would soon know about it. The word went out and in a day or two everything had gone. If one lived in a block of flats in town, one knew early in the morning, through the grapevine, in which flat there was bacon for sale, who had some butter, who had flour or grain and what was required in exchange. Everyone was involved and the system made survival possible.

The women in the coach were typical smugglers. They all had strong limbs and broad shoulders necessary for carrying loads which they would never have dreamed of carrying in peacetime. They were talking among themselves, mainly about their experiences in 'travelling', about prices, the best routes to be taken and the hard work of trying to earn a living with Germans all around. They did not seem to be worried about who overheard them. They laughed as they chattered about the stupidity and narrow-mindedness of the Germans, about their families, about life and its problems. The young man remained aloof, smoking a cigarette and looking on with some amusement.

At the first stop there was a commotion on the platform; the doors burst open and two gendarmes barged into the coach. The nondescript man shifted in his seat and opened his jacket slightly. A piece of paper appeared in his hand. The elegant young man remained as he was. '*Aufmachen, aufmachen*' shouted the gendarmes and all the bundles, baskets and sacks were thrown on to the floor and undone. To the intense satisfaction of the gendarmes, rings of sausages, sides of bacon, bottles of moonshine spirit and pats of butter were

7

revealed. They were snatched up and passed round. The women were left standing, livid with rage but speechless.

The gendarmes then turned to me. They ordered me to open my small, battered suitcase and probed into my most precious possession—a rolled blanket made of sheepskin. They found nothing of interest. The nondescript man had no luggage, so he showed them the piece of paper which he held in his hand. It seemed to satisfy them. At last they turned to the elegant young man and ordered him to open his suitcase. He did so, explaining in faultless German that he was a geologist and carried some geological samples which he had to deliver to a laboratory. If they proved to be what he thought they were, the Reich would be independent of Spain for the supply of sulphur. And there, at the top of the open suitcase, among some beautiful linen shirts and gaudy pyjamas, there lay a bundle of yellowish chunks of some metal, wrapped in strong brown paper. The Germans seemed quite impressed by the scientific jargon spoken in impeccable German, and after a perfunctory look at the garments in the suitcase they saluted and started to gather up the loot taken from the women. By this time the train was already pulling up at the next stop. The gendarmes left; a whistle went and the train started again.

The passengers were left in silence, a silence loaded with hatred and despair. After a while, however, their feelings seemed to change to envy and resentment, and the women turned against the young man, elegant, well-dressed and composed, calmly smoking a cigarette, seemingly without a care in the world.

'Yes,' an old woman muttered. 'Some people have all the luck.'

'Yes. They don't lose anything, do they?'

'They don't care. They have all the luck.'

'If only we were well-dressed and carried pigskin suitcases and had been taught to speak good German, we would probably get away without seeing our food whisked away to a German canteen.'

The grumbling went on and on, a continuous crescendo of resentment. As it grew, it was transformed into a blind hatred of all and sundry, but of the young man in particular. I could see that it was beginning to affect the young man and eventually, in a kind of comic desperation, he stood up and addressed them:

'You are all Poles, living under terror and oppression. People are killed every day for nothing, are deprived of their livelihood, put into the concentration camps, are beaten up and tortured for nothing. And here you are, cursing and hating me because I escaped any requisition and lost nothing. You should rejoice at my good fortune. You have lost your goods. I could easily have lost mine. And here they are.'

He opened his suitcase. Beneath his pyjamas and shirts they could see a sort of radio, fitting snugly into the bottom of the suitcase.

'Here are my goods,' he said. 'A radio transmitter for communication with London. And here is my pass.'

He opened his overcoat. The butt of a well-used Parabellum was showing over his belt. From his pockets he took out two hand grenades.

'Here you are. Do you still envy me? I am getting out at the next stop. Let no one dare to leave the carriage. I will be well covered at the next stop. So wait.'

A stunned silence fell on the company. There was fear and shame on every face.

I said nothing. I could well understand the young man's feelings but I felt that he was rather foolish. Too much had been at stake.

The train stopped. The young man jumped out and soon disappeared. Suddenly the women rushed towards the doors of the carriage. They were stopped in their tracks by the nondescript man who had produced a pass for the Germans. He had another sort of pass in his hand now, an ugly-looking 9mm Mauser. He waved them back to their seats. 'No one leaves the train at this station,' he said calmly. And nobody did.

9

The train started again. It was now running beside a small river, between pine trees dappled with golden light. Bars of sunshine danced and glinted between the trees.

After about twenty minutes the train stopped at Ostrowiec. The day was wonderfully quiet and warm, with the sun beating down from the cloudless sky.

A few soldiers and civilians left the two 'Nur für Deutsche' (Germans only) coaches. The two other fourth-class coaches disgorged about a dozen people, most of them carrying empty sacks. The district was rich in grain and cattle and supplied illicit food for quite a number of places, including Warsaw about a hundred and twenty miles away.

I was the last to make for the exit. I had a game leg and could not hurry. In my left hand I had my small battered suitcase with my shaving kit and a change of underwear. In my right I had my sheepskin blanket, warm in winter, cool in summer. A 'Wis' pistol, the most wonderfully balanced of all the guns I knew, was tucked snugly into my belt. In my breast pocket I had a 'Cockrel' sachet for headaches. It looked normal, except that the powder it contained had enough potassium cyanide added to kill a horse.

There was a ticket collector at the barrier and beside him a civilian, definitely Semitic. While I was surrendering my ticket, the civilian unobtrusively felt inside the bundle of my blanket with his hand. An agent? And a Jew?

I left the station, turning towards the main road. On my right the road turned sharply to the left, running due east. On my left, after the level crossing and running beside a steel mill, the road ran straight, sloping slightly upwards to the Market Square which could be seen in the distance with a few stalls on the pavement.

Across the road there was a cluster of half-grown trees and near it, partly hidden from the road by a hedge, a wooden bench. I crossed the road, sat on the bench, lit a cigarette and began to wait. I had been told to wait for six white ducks which would appear from the direction of the workers' dwellings, would cross the level crossing and go and wait at the entrance to the steel mill for the 5 pm hooter. I was told to follow a man who would then leave the mill, followed by the ducks. This man would lead me to my contact.

I looked in a leisurely fashion at the scene around me. As usual there was the feeling that life was going on at two separate levels. Everyone and everything bearing the mark of Germany was going by unacknowledged, rejected by everyone's consciousness. The civilians all seemed to know each other, acknowledging their meeting by a movement of the head or a wave of a hand. The town seemed to be saturated with German soldiers, well fed and clothed, displaying with every step the knowledge that they were the masters, not only of Poland, but also of most of Europe.

My cigarette had burnt out. It was five to five. Suddenly I saw them: six white ducks waddling in an orderly manner towards the steel mill. Nobody paid any attention to them.

They crossed the level crossing and at five o'clock sharp they were standing at the mill gate. The end-of-shift hooter went off, the gate opened and, clucking with joy, the ducks started to follow a tall, elderly man who emerged from the mill. The little company re-crossed the level crossing and I watched them enter the second entrance of the first house on the estate. That was it, I thought. But experience had taught me never to take things for granted. There was a tobacconist's kiosk nearby, so I went to buy some cigarettes. In the kiosk was a man of about thirty.

'Everything seems to be quite in Ostrowiec today,' I remarked.

'Yes, indeed. Too quiet for my liking,' was the answer.

'What do you mean?'

'Well, these blasted Germans seem to have everything sewn up. Nothing and nobody seems to bother them. But things will change soon, you wait and see.'

'You are very outspoken with a stranger. What if I reported you to the Germans?'

'You are all right. If you were not you would not have been checked out by the Gestapo agent.'

'You mean the Jewish chap at the station? How do you know that he checked on me?'

'It was Dr Spiegel. He has been their agent and informer from the start of the Occupation. This is why he is free to go where he pleases and, being a doctor with an extensive practice, he has done in quite a few of us. But why do you ask all these questions? What is your business in Ostrowiec?'

'I am just a businessman,' I answered. 'According to my information there is a lot of wheat flour to be had from the right quarters in Opatow. I am just waiting to thumb a lift there.'

'You seem to know what you are doing. But you must excuse me; it is my closing time and I must be off.'

The man left the kiosk, locked it up, said goodbye and went off towards the housing estate.

Things will change soon indeed, I thought. The news of my appointment must have been leaked somewhere along the line. And we called it 'the conspiracy'!

I was here to take over command of the Opatow District, known to be as dead as a doornail, where arrest followed arrest, and where the spirit of the people seemed to have been broken. That was the official version of what it was like there. The Regional Chief of Staff had warned me about the situation but believed that it would suit my temperament and aptitudes. Nobody else wanted the job, which did not seem very complimentary from my point of view!

The Chief of Staff said that the C.O. of the District had asked to be relieved of his job, believing that he was already blown. I would be on my own: no need to consult him, the Chief of Staff, about methods of carrying on the fight against the Germans. The Chief of Staff, originally from the River Prypet flotilla, was a graduate of the Staff College and used to say that when counting a flock of sheep he was taught to count all the legs and then divide by four.

'Felix,' he used to say, 'the difference between you and me is that you are counting heads only.'

Who was it who saw the checking of the blanket bundle at the station and how could this information have been transmitted so quickly to the man in the kiosk? And why? And who was the man at the kiosk?

Well, I said to myself, I shall soon know.

After the man had left I walked towards the second entrance of the estate. The ducks were nowhere to be seen. I went in and eventually I saw them on the first landing. I knocked at the door. It was opened by a young man of medium height with a swarthy complexion. We exchanged passwords. The suitcase and the blanket were taken from me and I was ushered into the dining-cum-sitting room of the flat which was simply but comfortably furnished.

'I am Joe M. But call me Joe, please. And you are the new C.O.?

'Yes,' I answered. 'I am.'

'We shall now eat. Maria,' he yelled, 'bring the food, please.'

A girl entered the room carrying a tray. She was a beauty— dark, shapely, with brown eyes and a strong mouth.

'Now, sir,' said Joe, 'Maria is my sister and she is the one who knows everyone and everything that is going on in Ostrowiec. She knows who is working for the Organization, in what capacity, and where everybody works and lives. She is a teacher by profession and is a good judge of character.'

Maria stood in front of me and looked me over. After a while she looked into my eyes. Time ceased to exist. She seemed to probe deep into my consciousness and sub-consciousness, and I suddenly realized that I had l'éternel féminin in front of me: the synthesis in one woman, as it were, of all the attributes of innumerable generations of women—the ability to love and to hate, to suffer and to rejoice, the determination to live and the will to fight. These have been the principle characteristics of Polish women

13

throughout the whole history of the nation.

Her eyes lit up with unexpected warmth. She relaxed, gripped my hand and shook it.

'Welcome, sir, to Ostrowiec,' she said. 'We shall be glad to help you.'

The initial wariness had vanished.

'The organization here seems to be a family affair,' I said.

'To some extent, yes,' answered Maria. 'It must be so. We have been on our own for so long. We have not seen much of the C.O. all these years and if we do anything, which is not much, we do it on second-hand information, as it were.'

I felt uneasy. I was at a loss what to say.

'You are all right,' said Maria with a smile.

'Thank you,' I said. 'Now, this is the schedule for this evening and for tomorrow. If I can stay with you for the night it would be nice. We shall eat and I shall go to bed early. I have had a hard journey and must have some rest. For tomorrow I would like to have the following matters arranged: first, find me a safe house; second, I must have a bicycle to be able to move around the district. You may have noticed that I am not good at making long journeys on foot; third, arrange a meeting with the retiring C.O. if and when you can. We shall see what to do next as we go on. By the way, do you know the man at the cigarette kiosk near the level crossing? Oh, and where are the white ducks?'

'The man at the kiosk,' Maria answered, 'is one of us. Perhaps one day you will get to know him personally. As to the ducks, they belong to my father. He raised them from the time they hatched, and they adopted him as their mother. Everybody knows them and even the Germans have accepted their wandering to and from the steel mill. They always go with my father to the mill in the morning and for three years now have not missed a single day in greeting him at the mill entrance at the end of his shift.'

We all relaxed. The food was simple but good. I asked Joe if he minded me having my pistol with me. Joe, however, said that he would prefer to put it away in the ducks' pen. This he did and the three of us relaxed and went off to sleep, Maria in her own room, Joe and I in another bedroom.

I was not a very evangelical Christian. However, I firmly believed in God, the God who had guided me throughout my childhood during the Great Russian Revolution and during the two years of this war. During the Revolution I had several times escaped unscathed through a hail of bullets. In 1939, and later on, I had several miraculous escapes, first from the Russians and then from the Germans. I knew that my life was not in the hands of men, but of God, and so every evening I first used to thank God for the day just passed and then commit to Him my safe sleep and the day ahead. I did this now and we all went to sleep, the only sounds coming through the closed windows being those of occasional German lorries rumbling through the street outside. We slept.

III

The Takeover

THE NEXT FEW days I spent on my own during the daytime. Maria was trying unsuccessfully to contact the retiring C.O., a certain Major P. Joe was arranging for me to have a bicycle as my primary means of transport, and was looking for one or two safe houses for those occasions when I would have to stay in Ostrowiec. As a result I had plenty of time to take stock of the situation and to familiarize myself with the terrain.

The District of Opatow, in which Ostrowiec was situated, was one of the most fertile regions of Poland. The town of Ostrowiec, with a population of about 30,000, was the biggest and the most industrialized in the region. It was built astride the River Kamienna, which flowed east. The main road leading from the west, from another industrial town, Starachowice, was metalled, and in Ostrowiec, after passing the Gestapo HQ, ran straight into the market square. In the middle of the square it turned sharply to the right, then downhill past the barracks of the Gendarmerie towards the river, with the steel mill just across the level crossing. After the level crossing, at the workers' housing estate, the road turned sharply east, going through the suburb of Ludwikow, after which it divided, one road going east, the other one south towards Opatow.

North of Ostrowiec there was a vast pine and spruce forest, with one dirt road leading north. All the other tracks leading to the scattered farms in the forest were of sand and no car or lorry could possibly use any of them.

16

The terrain east of Ostrowiec was flat as far as the River Vistula, with one bridge and one ford across it. There was one small town, Ozarow, about ten kilometres from the river.

About fifteen kilometres from Ostrowiec was the District Administrative Centre of Opatow, a town of about 10,000 inhabitants. The soil south of Ostrowiec was a fertile loess, the landscape intersected by unmetalled secondary roads, with the main, made-up road leading from Ostrowiec to Opatow and then further to the south-east to the town of Sandomierz on the Vistula. All roads between the villages ran along deep ravines, cut into the loess by generations of farm-carts; they were rock-hard in dry weather, deep mud when wet, and filled with snow in winter.

Protruding into the south-west corner of the district were the Swietokrzyskie (Holy Cross) Mountains, an alluvial range of rocks, up to 1000 metres high, covered with spruce and larch forests. The range had three passes running from north to south. These passes were on the historic route from the Baltic Sea to the south.

South of the mountain range ran the dirt road linking Opatow with Kielce, the provincial capital of the province of Kielce. Another road from Opatow led south-west to the towns of Bogorya and Staszow. All except the main roads were impassable for trucks and cars, and seemed to present possibilities for hit-and-run jobs when necessary.

I could now start to consider my job in more detail. The ultimate objective of my Organization Z.W.Z. (the Armed Fight Alliance), transformed eventually into the Home Army (A.K.), was to prepare an armed uprising at such a time as the German Army would begin to disintegrate before the final collapse of the Third Reich, due to the victorious advance of the Allies. This idea seemed to be quite reasonable, except that nobody in the High Command of the Home Army seemed to have considered what part the Russians would play. They surely would not be idle. I knew them. I had lived through the

17

Great Revolution of 1917 and I knew a few things about the aims of Russian Communism and their methods. I was still only a child when the hatred of the Bolsheviks towards everyone and everything representing the Western way of life had become clear to me. At the age of eight I went to see the headquarters of the Tcheka in Kiev and I saw walls covered with human brains and drains in the stables full of congealed human blood. Even now I could remember the rumbling of lorries at night, their horns blaring to drown the groans and cries of the half-dead bodies being taken to the mass graves. I was caught up in the Russian invasion of the country in 1939. I knew what had happened to the Polish intelligentsia caught in their advance. My parents managed to escape to Hungary. My family and I just managed to escape to the German side of Occupied Poland. I was arrested by the Germans in November, 1939, and escaped from a military hospital in February, 1940. I had made all the necessary arrangements to rejoin the Polish Navy in Great Britain (I was a lieutenant, executive branch). I was, however, ordered to stay in Poland.

Then I had a narrow escape. I was going to the house at which I had to make my contact. It was in a quiet street. Each house had a garden in front. The street was absolutely empty. There was no sign of life. I did not like it. Something made me turn round and go to buy some cigarettes at the nearby kiosk.

'It is very quiet,' I said to the man, lighting a cigarette.

'Yes,' said the man. 'No wonder. In that house over there the Gestapo are sitting.'

The house he pointed towards was the house I was going to. That was the day of the first mass arrests of members of the Underground. The staff was in complete disarray. Most of their covers had been blown and I was ordered to stay and take over communications.

My grandmother, a Russian, had said to me at the start of the war, 'Remember, my boy, that, whatever happens, the Russians, not the Germans, will be your ultimate foes. They will present the main problem to the Polish nation.'

18

She was right. Half of Poland was under the Russians. Millions were being deported to Siberia, shot or imprisoned. On the German side of divided Poland, the Communists were lying low. But I knew that they were trying to get hold of as many arms as possible. Much had been buried, or just abandoned during the 1939 débâcle. What for?

I was warned that apathy and defeatism were rife in the Opatow District. Thousands of deportees from that part of Poland incorporated into the Reich were swelling the population. They had to be fed and housed. I had to be the provider. The Germans, feeling secure, were exerting pressure on farmers and landowners to provide the required levies of corn, beef, pork, sugar and other foodstuffs. These levies were determined according to the highly developed standards of German agriculture and were ridiculously high by local standards. A strange nation, I thought. With the true German appreciation of the word '*Ordnung*', they were taking care of the forests, were supplying fertilisers, cheap spirit, cigarettes, boots and other clothing to the farmers against the deliveries of the levies. The quantities were minimal, but the stuff was being supplied. The town dwellers, on the other hand, had starvation rations. Yet, they too managed to survive. How, is quite a story. They did it by pilfering from the German depots, by falsifying ration cards and by black-market deals. Some of them lived quite well, even made money. Everything was fair game since everything belonged to the Germans. The Germans were, however, like babes compared to the Russians. *Befehl ist Befehl* (an order is an order) and when ordered to look, for instance, for moonshine vodka, they would look for vodka only, as ordered.

I remember one of the couriers I had met the year before in the street of Kielce. She was dragging a huge suitcase behind her, visibly shaken and quite pale.

'What happened to you?' I asked.

'Nothing, thank God. Do you know what I have in this suitcase?'

19

'Well, you come from Warsaw, where you were to get some newsheets.'

'Yes. The suitcase is full of them. Our luggage was searched on the train. The gendarme opened my suitcase, had a perfunctory look at the contents and left me half dead with fright.' They were looking for smuggled alcohol and vodka, the time being near Easter. They had no orders to look for anything else, so they didn't.

Open action against the Germans seemed very far away. As far as *any* action was concerned, I had my own views. I remembered the first hundred Poles shot near Warsaw in the autumn of 1939 for the killing, in the pub brawl, of a German soldier. I remembered the stupid behaviour and silly bravura actions of the self-styled upholder of Polish independence and military honour, the so-called Major Hubala, who had been operating in the spring of 1940 in the forests of the Kielce Province. He killed a few Germans and made a few demonstrations of his strength—his force consisted of about a hundred cut-throats. I had been directly involved, with other members of the Staff of the Province, in trying to persuade him to abandon his activities, but with no success. The result was total extermination for the population of two villages. More than two thousand Poles, men, women and children, had been brutally murdered in graves they had to dig themselves. The Polish people had already suffered heavy losses—in battles in the army; on roads by air strafing; en masse during the defence of Warsaw in 1939; deported to Siberia; taken to the concentration camps. No nation could survive such losses, and they were by no means the last. I therefore felt very deeply that any killing of Germans could be justified only if such a killing would in the balance show a net gain to the population. Gestapo—yes, when necessary; informers—yes, they were traitors and instrumental in many deaths: even then, only if a careful balance could be established. I felt that it would take courage, persuasion and authority to impose such a point of view, especially on young people, who would have to be kept in check. It is so easy to kill without giving any thought to the consequences.

Morale, I thought, would have to be boosted somehow. This, I decided, could be done by making a clean sweep of all the informers working for the Gestapo. If cleverly done, it would leave little leeway for the Gestapo to act. After all, both informers and Gestapo knew the possibilities. All the time I would have to increase the better-knit units of the members of the Organization; to provide these units with arms, at least to let them know that the arms existed and would be ready for use when needed; to provide for the families of members killed in action, or arrested in the line of duty; to provide instruction in guerrilla and subversive warfare; to let them all realize that somewhere there was someone who cared.

Funds, therefore, would be needed. I was not yet sure, but I felt that the landowners would be most likely to provide these funds. After all they all had the possibility of making vast amounts of money by divering part of their produce on to the black market.

Having been on the staff of the Regional (Provincial) Command, I knew very well that the subsidies from Warsaw were reaching only the headquarters of the Provincial Command, and that only very small amounts would occasionally go to the districts. My own personal subsidy for one month was just enough to buy, say, two kilos of butter, on the black market. When on the staff of the Provincial Headquarters I had gone hungry most of the time. To obtain rations now I would have to procure new identity papers. The Polish police in Kielce were looking for a certain Mr Krechowski (my official surname), suspected of running a brothel. Brothels had been established for the German Armed Services only and at the time I had been in charge of Communications, a job which required the use of, and meeting with, many girls. That was the reason why I was travelling with a pistol as a means of identification as I had had no time, on my transfer, to obtain a new set of identification papers.

21

The Germans; informers; the boosting of morale; arms; funds; safe houses for myself and, if necessary, for members of my staff; transport; and, last but not least, staffing: these were the immediate problems which I would have to tackle.

At last Joe brought a bicycle. It had no gears and no brakes, but it could be ridden. The next day Maria brought the news that the retiring C.O., Major P. was waiting for me near the town of Opatow, at the home of 'Dahlia', the owner of an estate near Opatow, whose husband was fighting with the Carpathian Polish Brigade at Tobruk.

I had not ridden a bicycle for about ten years. With some misgivings I mounted it and, guided by Joe on another bicycle, off we went, using the narrow smugglers' footpaths criss-crossing the countryside.

The house was a typical Polish country house, small but well kept, set in a beautiful garden.

'Dahlia' was beautiful and had style. I was invited to take a seat and she disappeared. After a few minutes she came back with a tall, gaunt man.

'I am Major P.,' he said. 'I am glad to see you.'

He had a haunted look. His eyelids were twitching and his hands restless.

'A "muslim",' I thought.

The name 'muslim' was given in the concentration camps to people who had lost hope. A young man, strong and healthy, used to last about three weeks if he was a 'muslim'. On the other hand, old, frail, sick people, determined to live, with the indefinable characteristic of inner strength, seemed to last for ever.

I could get virtually nothing from the Major. There was no discussion; there was no talk about anything. The Major left after a few minutes. And that was the way I took over the command of the district of Opatow.

The day was, however, well spent. At lunch, served by a butler, I managed to induce Dahlia to become the chief fund-raiser and to preside over a committee, which she would form,

22

which would supervise the spending of the money raised. Myself or my staff were to supply detailed sums of money required for the efficient operation of the Organization, along lines laid down by me. The finance committee would discuss the problems and thus everybody giving their money for the cause would know for what it was intended. In future money, the source of so many evils, would not, I hoped, concern me any more. Dahlia promised to start work straightaway. I did not ask how she intended to do it and I left the security of the job to her.

She also introduced me to her steward, a peasant's son who lived on the estate and had contacts in all the villages around Opatow. The day ended with a swearing-in ceremony for Dahlia, her cousins Maria and Alec, and the steward.

I slept at the steward's home and next day Dahlia took me to Opatow, to the only miller in town, Roman Niewojt, with whom she had many illicit corn and flour transactions.

Roman already had about twenty daredevils organized. He had plenty of money and, above all, was very friendly with, indeed had in his pocket, Herr Donat, the Chief of SD (*Sicherheists Dienst*) for the District! Donat longed only to go back to Hamburg to his old job as a teacher. He had a tacit agreement with Roman: if kept in funds he would do his best to ensure that the town of Opatow and the district surrounding it would be quiet and secure, a good place for all to live.

After sending word of my whereabouts to Maria in Ostrowiec, I stayed in Opatow for a week. I had also met and sworn in a cousin of Roman's, Stanislas, who had been an Inspector for the Ministry of Agriculture before the war and was retained in an inspector's capacity by Baron von Böninghausen, the *Kreislandwirt*. In his job Stan was able to travel all over the District at any time without raising any suspicions. He always travelled on foot, although walking was torture to him. He had a kind of corn on his toes, rooted deeply between the joints, which caused him agonizing pain

23

all the time he walked. After some discussion, I offered him the job of a roving liaison-cum-organizing officer. Stan accepted the job quite willingly.

I gladly accepted a gift from Roman of a pair of sturdy riding boots, made to measure by a reliable cobbler, a member of the Opatow team. The identity passes (*Kennkarte*) were being issued by the *Kreishauptmann*'s (Chief Administrator of the District) Office in Opatow. The clerk dealing with the passes was one of Roman's men. They decided to present the new *Kennkarte* for the *Kreishauptmann*'s signature together with as many others as possible. The new identity card would have to be on an official blank, the supply of which was kept at the Town Hall. This was necessary because of their special markings and it was simpler to have an official one from the Town Hall than to use one from the printers direct. The photograph was taken by one of Roman's men, the negative destroyed. The new *Kennkarte* was duly signed by the *Kreishauptmann*, no questions asked, and delivered to me withing five days.

A safe house had also been found. It was at the flat of an old, but very active and popular, midwife. She used to be on the nursery staff of the late Czar Nicholas II of Russia at Tsarskoe Selo. The flat was more or less in the middle of the town and, since she had many clients, a few more visitors would not attract any undue interest. At the first breakfast I had with her, I was stirring sugar in my ersatz coffee with a twenty-two-carat gold spoon, presented to her husband after a supper at the Czar's table.

Another safe house had been found for me at the home of two distant cousins of Roman, bachelors with a smallholding on the road from Opatow to Kielce. Wherever I stayed for the night I was always offered food. For this I was glad, because my upkeep funds were very low. The *Kennkarte* was in the name of Witold Szymanski, a teacher from Pomerania. Every tenth Pole was a Szymanski. I also decided to have another pseudonym for use in the District. Retaining my old name of

Felix for correspondence with the Provincial C.O., I chose for internal use that of Tarlo, an historical name associated with the District.

By now my identity was officially known to eleven people and I realized that, in fact, many more people already knew about me. The grapevine was in all probability working at full speed. I also realized that the security of all would depend on each one of the people involved. I was, however, confident of my judgement of people. In my talks with all of them I stressed the necessity of avoiding loose talk. I also knew that the security of all concerned would depend to a large extent on the identification, and if necessary on the liquidation, of all traitors and informers. I knew that I would have, as a matter of urgency, to try to penetrate the German establishment itself at all possible levels. With all this in mind I took leave of all in Opatow and cycled back to Ostrowiec to Joe's place.

Maria was at home. She took me to new safe lodgings which she had found for me. The house was situated in the suburbs, very near the railway line. Since the line was regularly patrolled by the army and the patrols passed within a few yards of the house, I felt that I would be quite secure. No sabotage or any unusual doings would be permitted in the vicinity, and there would be no reason for the Gestapo or Gendarmerie to investigate the house, which was under the very eyes, as it were, of the army. Unless, of course . . .

The landlady was not an active member of the Organization. Maria had known her from childhood and was sure of her patriotism. Nevertheless, a cover had to be provided, and Maria decided that the best one would be that of a member of a smuggling syndicate. This would explain my absences. It provided the woman, however, with an excuse to ask for a substantial rent, which I could in no way afford. I started to haggle, whimpering about the hard times, the family I had to provide for, the danger and losses.

With Maria's support, we managed to cut the rent by half. Nevertheless, after it was paid I was left nearly penniless. But I

25

was accustomed to going hungry, and I also knew that wherever I went I would get food. I knew too, from experience, that this food was always accompanied by a lot of moonshine vodka. People always went out of their way to provide the best for guests like me. There was in consequence a real danger of becoming an alcoholic. To refuse was often taken as an offence. So one had to drink. Sadly, I loathed the stuff!

I left my food coupons with the landlady. I asked her to dry my ration of bread. It was good to be able to munch some dried bread when going hungry to bed.

When the landlady had left, I had a long talk with Maria. I asked her about people, businesses in the town and official institutions. Her knowledge of the town folk was amazing. She could assess the character of scores of people. She could detail their connections, habits, social activities and interests. Three men looked rather promising for the kind of job they would be called upon to do. One was a certain Mr S., the Director of the local branch of the so-called RGO (the main Commission for the Care of Refugees), an institution officially sponsored by the Germans, with head offices in Cracow under a Pole, Baron Ronikier. The refugees were displaced people from the part of Poland incorporated into the Third Reich. In his official capacity, S. had to be in constant touch with the German administration and with the refugees. His pre-war occupation had been as an Inspector of Secondary Education and his record was good. He lived on the outskirts of Ostrowiec, with the back of his house just touching the forest north of the town. The forest was of dense pine. Its soil was sandy and impassable to cars and lorries. His house made a good meeting place. S. had already been working with the previous C.O., Major P.

Next there was a certain Peter T., codename Blackie. He also had many connections in the town and in the district. His close friend and colleague was a teacher, John. Although his usefulness could be immense, he had been, until now, left virtually inoperative.

The third man to be considered was quite young, aged twenty-four, son of the Notary Public in Ostrowiec, working in his father's office. According to Maria this young man, codename Drake, already had the nucleus of a counter-intelligence staff, which, given the proper stimulus and directives, could prove really useful.

Maria also mentioned an underground cell at Cmielow, a small town or large village about ten kilometres outside Ostrowiec on the main road leading east. For centuries Cmielow had been famous for its porcelain.

The talk with Maria lasted a long time, well into the night. I found myself turning over and over the information she had somehow stored in her pretty head. There was one fundamental problem upon which I had to decide. If I chose my staff from the people discussed with Maria, she would, sooner or later, know about everyone and everything, and would be the weak link in the chain of command. What would happen if she was arrested? Did Maria realize the danger of knowing too much? On the other hand, I thought, there can be no real secrecy in the countryside. Under the German yoke everyone knows everything about everyone else, a matter of simple survival. I put my doubts bluntly to Maria.

I felt very humble in the face of Maria's response. I watched a small, beautiful girl become the epitome of Polish womanhood, who over the centuries, as the nation fought its enemies on every border, had given her life and her loved ones in the cause of freedom.

'Sir,' she said, 'you may rest assured that whatever happens to me, whatever they do to me if I am arrested, they will obtain no information from me. I have my special means of avoiding the necessity to talk. Believe me.'

I looked at her for a long time. She was beautiful; she was young; she had character; and she was also a woman. I saw in her eyes a quiet determination and certitude of purpose in life. I became convinced in my own mind that there was no other alternative but to pray, and to believe, and to have faith in her.

27

There was no need for further words. I made Maria my personal messenger and asked her to arrange, as soon as possible, a meeting with S., Drake and Blackie at S.'s house. Maria left.

It was already curfew time. The landlady came back with some bread and margarine. I accepted with gratitude a glass of milk, ate a slice of bread with margarine and went to bed.

Before falling asleep I prayed. I thanked God for the day, for everything I had been able to do during the day, and I thanked Him for the bread and milk. I thanked Him for all the people who were willing to risk their lives fighting Evil. I prayed for my parents, somewhere in Europe, I prayed for my wife Irena and my son Andrew, staying not far away with my cousin. I prayed for my friend Felix, whose name I was carrying in my work and who had disappeared, taken in September, 1939, by the Russians. I prayed for insight into human nature. I prayed that the decisions I would have to take would be the right ones. After finishing with the Lord's Prayer I went to sleep.

I slept well. In the morning I had some bread and a glass of goat's milk. I had a talk with the landlady. The talk proved to be quite useful. I gained an insight into living conditions in the town and the attitude of the Germans as she saw it. I learned indirectly who could and who could not be trusted. I was told quite a lot about the Communists in the town, their attitude and their activities; about prices on the black market and the centres of illegal food supplies. My landlady proved to be quite a woman in her own way. She talked freely and did not ask a single question. She must have been warned about me. I felt quite at ease with her. Army patrols passed by every two hours. She was on nodding terms with nearly all of them, which was reassuring.

In the afternoon I took the bike and went to look for the house of S. Maria was waiting at the garden gate. No one else was in sight. I followed Maria into the house, where three men were waiting. Maria introduced me, showing them a slip of paper, the official message from Provincial H.Q. confirming my appointment as the new C.O. of the Home Army of Opatow District. There were no queries; all three men accepted it as genuine.

The oldest of the three, a small man with greying hair and a moustache, was S.; the second was tall and of swarthy complexion—Blackie; the youngest was Drake, a man about twenty-four, blond, with bright blue eyes.

After a while we were all at ease. S. was the most self-confident. He seemed to know everyone. He had been born and bred in Ostrowiec and had spent all his life in the town. As the director of the local branch of RGO he was in contact with the refugees from the west and also with the German authorities. S. suggested that he could get a good cover for me. A friend of his, a seed merchant, needed a Sugar-Beet Inspector. The position would have to be approved by the Agriculture Department of Governor-General Frank's office in Cracow. S. had a friend in this department and, if I could provide a photograph of myself, he could arrange for me to be issued with an official pass, which would enable me to move freely, not only within the District but well beyond it. A Sugar-Beet Inspector had to check all sugar-beet plantations for possible contamination by the beet used as cattle fodder.

Was there a trustworthy photographer in the town? Yes, said Drake. I gladly accepted the arrangement. During these deliberations Blackie was quiet and unassuming. Whatever he had to say made sense.

Drake had shown himself to be a man of action. Without any orders or prompting from his former C.O., he had established the following contacts who accepted him as their superior:

1. The postmaster. He, in his turn, had several of his men working for him, employed at the sorting office. All post addressed to the Gestapo, Gendarmerie and German officials could be, and was, checked and, if necessary, suppressed.

2. The chief of the telephone exchange. He had the exchange covered by his men. All telephone calls to the Gestapo,

Gendarmerie, etc., were monitored and an alarm system had been established.

3. Through a very intricate chain of intermediaries Drake had been asked by the secretary to *Sturmbannführer* Soldau, chief of the District Gestapo, for official approval by the Underground authorities for her to become Soldau's mistress as well as his secretary. Soldau was head-over-heels in love with her. She wanted to settle a few scores with the Germans. To become his mistress, a fact which would soon be known to everyone, she had to have the blessing of the Underground. Without it she would be an outcast for ever.

According to enquiries carried out by Drake, she was a Pole of German descent and was married to a Polish officer, a prisoner-of-war in Germany. In line with their policy of trying to induce as many Poles of German origin as possible to become so-called *Volksdeutsche* (who had all the prerogatives and privileges of *Reichsdeutsche*, while residing in the General Gouvernement), the Germans had promised to release her husband if she signed the necessary documents. She so loved her husband that, without giving much thought to the consequences, she had signed and straightaway was handed a special ration card and could claim all sorts of priorities over Polish families. What she did not reckon with was that her son had to enrol in the Hitler Youth movement. He was a boy of twelve and hated all Germans. But in his innocence he rather enjoyed the military drill, the parades, etc. One evening, together with one of his friends, another non-voluntary *Volksdeutsche* and *Hitler Jugend* member, he was in charge of the cloakroom at a dance for Germans in the town of Czestochowa. The guests left their overcoats and belts, complete with pistols, in the cloakroom and after the dance was well under way the two boys, hidden behind the racks of overcoats, began to examine the pistols and discuss which type could be best used for killing Germans, describing to each other the gory details of the imagined killings. This talk was overheard by a late arrival, a Gestapo man. Without much ado he shot both boys dead.

30

When the mother came to fetch her son home she found him on the floor with his head blown to pieces.

In the meantime, while the mother was still with the body of her son, the husband came home, released from the PoW camp. Since he did not find his family at home he started to make enquiries among the neighbours and very soon learned that his wife had become, and was now, a *Volksdeutsche* and that his son was a member of the *Hitler Jugend*. He went home and promptly hanged himself in the drawing room. When the wife came home with the body of their son, she found her husband hanging dead from the chandelier.

There were some loose ends in her history. Apparently she nearly went mad, and no wonder. She was in hospital (reserved for Germans) for a few weeks, but somehow did not lose face with the Germans and was officially transferred to Ostrowiec, where she was to work at one of the German offices. There she met Soldau. According to all available information she was bent on revenge, and when offered the job as personal secretary to the Gestapo chief, she eagerly accepted the position. The job proved to be more than that of a secretary, because Soldau was enthusiastic in his endeavours to become her lover. And that was where she thought she would exercise her revenge, by passing to the Underground all the information she could lay her hands on.

After some discussion I wrote in my own handwriting (my natural handwriting was vertical; all documents related to my work I tried to write in a different, slanting longhand) the following note:

Ostrowiec, May 1941

To whom it may concern:

This is to certify that all activities, whether private or official, have been carried out by Mrs. M. with the full knowledge and approval of the Home Army Command of the District of Opatow.

Signed

Tarlo, C.O. of District Opatow

If the document was to have any value in the future, a duplicate of it had to be kept somehow in the command archives. I had stressed the fact that all paper work had to be kept to a minimum. Some documents, nevertheless, would have to be kept and preserved. Drake suggested that he take care of all documents. He had prepared a virtually undetectable place for such items. We all agreed to use this place for the archives and to entrust both certificates to Drake for safekeeping.

S. agreed to be my second-in-command and to be responsible, *inter alia*, for all communications. He already knew the address of the mail box to the Provincial Command; he knew Roman, Maria and Joe and it was easy for him to organize the necessary communication service between me and the four or five centres of command I was eventually hoping to establish.

Blackie agreed to take care of all finance. He would work in close cooperation with Dahlia, she providing the funds and he explaining to her and her committee how the funds would be used, and presenting to her the budget (if one could discuss the budget of an underground organization). I had stipulated that no family of a man arrested or killed in action should be left without financial support and that quite a large proportion of available funds would have to be used for the supply of arms.

The High Command in Warsaw had issued an order that all arms hidden during the 1939 débâcle were to be surrendered on a voluntary, patriotic basis. This was, as usual, wishful thinking. In regions of Poland where large army units had to surrender, especially in regions like that of Opatow with huge forests and countryside difficult to negotiate by cars and lorries, huge amounts of arms had been left behind, and very quickly these arms had disappeared into barns, pigsties, church steeples and the like. Patriotism was undoubtedly alive, but it always seemed to be on the increase when supported with tangible evidence of money or other goods. People also wanted to know that the arms which they had hidden at the risk of their lives would be put to good use and not taken away by someone calling himself this or that. Communists were always prepared to pay good money for arms—fortunately without much success, Stalin being in league with Hitler.

I had to explain that I would not touch any of the money myself, even when it was needed for official purposes. All payments would have to be made through Blackie. Nobody, ever, would be given the opportunity to have any doubts as to the use of the money collected. Blackie and his friend John would be responsible.

As mentioned before, Drake already had an intelligence team in Ostrowiec, with a separate communication link with the Intelligence Officer of the Provincial Command. It remained for him to find a man who would be responsible for the intelligence in the rest of the District, to develop it to the furthest possible extent. I wanted to have information about all Gendarmerie patrols, about the appearance of any radio-location vehicles, about every arrest, Gestapo activities and so on. Last, but not least, Drake had to raise and organize an execution squad. Drake said that he already had someone chosen for the job.

The meeting was finished and I was glad to see the food coming from the kitchen: milk, bread, sausage and cottage cheese. I ate well that evening.

IV

The Cleaning-Up

FOR THE NEXT few weeks work in the District was in full swing. The District was becoming saturated by detachments of von Manstein's IV Panzer Army. All the roads were virtually blocked by lorries, troop-carriers and tanks. The German troops looked fresh, well-fed and proud. They were all being transferred from France. Discipline was strict, the Gestapo and SD were nowhere in sight and, funnily enough, I felt quite safe in my travels through the countryside. I and my staff were fully operational by now. Four other command executives had been established. Besides Opatow, I had appointed four other commanders: one at Ozarow, east of Ostrowiec on the River Vistula; one at Cmielow; one at Backowice, south of the Holy Cross Mountains, and one at Milejowice, north of the mountains. Everywhere I was met with respect. Everyone expected orders and decisions from me.

The *Feldgendarmerie* kept order everywhere, laughing at the amateurish attempts to sabotage troop movements by reversing sign-posts—youngsters trying their hand at sabotage.

The sub-command post at Cmielow was run by two brothers, employees in the china factory. They took me into a huge barn across the road from their home. The threshing floor of beaten earth held a huge cage with about two dozen rabbits in it. When the cage was moved from its place (it took a considerable effort), I could see a beautifully camouflaged

34

trap-door in the centre of the space, covering a narrow shaft with a ladder attached to the side. The bottom of the shaft opened into a small room, its walls reinforced by wooden beams. Along two sides of the room were racks containing seventy-five rifles. Two heavy machine-guns were on the floor, together with an 80-mm mortar, boxes of ammunition and one small table. All the equipment was in perfect condition, cleaned and oiled. Ventilation was provided through a duct leading from the ceiling to an empty bee-hive, which stood among a group of twenty occupied ones in the orchard outside the barn. I was happy. Not only had I access to some arms and ammunition but I had also found an ideal place for the radio transmitter, due to arrive shortly, which would provide communication from the Warsaw headquarters to London via Sweden.

The two brothers also showed me about a hundred bottles of gold solution, used for painting the chinaware. The solution was about thirty per cent gold, so that they had managed to conceal from the Germans some thirty kilos of pure gold.

One day Drake suggested that I see the newly appointed head of the execution squad. I was not very happy about the meeting, but I had to agree. I felt that, in the case of executions, I would have to take full responsibility, and exercise an absolute authority. With their usual wishful thinking, the High Command, since its establishment, had ordered the Provincial Commands to set up *Sady Kapturowe* (kangaroo courts), with a proper judge of the Polish Courts presiding, if possible. But what lawyer, let alone judge, would take the responsibility of sentencing someone to death on partial evidence only? To take any accused to a court so constituted was not, and could not be, a practical proposition and in effect any sentence passed by such a court would be nothing less than murder in the eyes of the law, and the judge would have to carry the responsibility for it before God and posterity. Few judges were still at liberty. I had the opportunity of approaching all the survivors at the time when I was on the Provincial

35

staff. None would agree to become judge of such a court, some on principle, some because they were afraid of the involvement, as was the case with one of my distant relatives. He had unfortunately agreed to serve on the panel of judges of the Court of Appeal set up by the Germans. This Court had, of course, no powers, but served only as a shield for the so-called 'legal' methods of the government controlled by Governor-General Frank.

I knew very well that in practice I would have to make all the decisions in this respect. Whether the High Command managed to institute such courts in the end I do not know. But I doubt it.

The meeting with Drake and Stas, the young man willing to act as liquidator or, putting it simply, to kill traitors and selected Germans, took place at a remote house near the forest with an easy escape route. Stas was about twenty-four, blond, built like an athlete, with broad shoulders, deep chest and powerful arms.

'Do you know anything about unarmed combat?' I asked.

'Yes. I know it from the army.'

'Have you ever killed a German except on the battlefield?'

'Yes. I had to kill four Germans after our Division had to lay down its arms. I was escaping while on my way to a PoW camp.'

'How did you kill them?'

'One by strangulation, one by knifing and two by shooting.'

'Are you a good shot, and do you know where to shoot to kill?'

'Yes. I was the best pistol shot in my regiment.'

'Are you prepared to kill a traitor or a German on my orders?'

'Yes. It will be a pleasure.'

I sighed. This is what war does to people. Stealing becomes a duty, killing a pleasure—or so the killers think, not realizing that any killing distorts one's mind and soul. If killing is not properly motivated, if it is carried out without compassion, this distortion gets out of proportion and eventually must destroy the killer psychologically.

'This is where you are mistaken, my boy.' (I was only a few years older than Stas). 'No killing should give you pleasure. It is an act which will be on your conscience for ever. I understand that you have been brought up as a Christian, and you should remember that God said, "Thou shalt not kill." If you survive this war, you will see in mental hospitals many men and women who learnt to kill with pleasure. We have the right to defend ourselves and those we love, and an obligation to protect others of our kind. This is the reason why we must kill if necessary. But, if we have to do it, we must do it with compassion, remembering that we are destroying life. It is not the same thing as killing in battle. Firstly, in battle you do not know whom you kill and secondly, you do not know whether or not you have actually been successful. In your job, which you have agreed to undertake, you will sometimes have to kill men or women whom you know. You will sometimes have to execute people as courageous as yourself. In their eyes you will see no hatred or fear, but acceptance of the fact that you have the upper hand. You should salute their courage. You will also meet men or women who, faced with death, will behave like terrified animals, licking your boots, vomiting and crying for pity. The task becomes much more difficult then. It will seem as if you are trying to kill a dog, as it crawls on its belly looking at you with terrified eyes. You must then do your job with pity, but without hesitation, secure in the knowledge that the decision was not yours. The decision will be always mine, and mine alone, and if we make a mistake, the burden of remorse and guilt will be borne by me, and only by me. I can only hope that I shall not make such a mistake. So, my boy, think about what I have said. I will meet you in a few days' time and I hope that you will not look forward to taking pleasure in your job. Dismiss.'

Stas left. I stayed with Drake to discuss the problem of

security and to go through all the evidence available concerning the activities of the known German agents. Drake presented well-documented evidence against two Poles, a certain Dr Spiegel and his assistant. They had been instrumental in nearly all the arrests carried out by the Gestapo during the previous two years. They openly boasted of carrying Gestapo identity cards; both were armed and were seen nearly every day to stay for long periods at Soldau's headquarters on the outskirts of the town, on the main road leading west to Starachowice. They had been spending a great deal of time in the company of Peters, Soldau's second-in-command, a bully and a Gestapo butcher. People had been aware for some time that Spiegel, who was a Jew, was closely involved with the Germans, and although his activities seemed to have ceased for the time being, all the same, as my organization began to expand its activities Spiegel and his assistant were bound to be a source of danger. Drake asked for a decision. I was unwilling, for the time being, to condemn them. I said that I would have to discuss the problem with S. and Blackie first. There was also Stas's attitude to be taken into account. In due course S. and Blackie agreed with me that the two men would have to go.

A week or so later I saw Stas again. The young man seemed to be somewhat subdued. He said that he had thought everything over and that he could see the truth in what I had said to him. He also told me that he had discussed the matter with a friend of his who would be his partner, that they had both gone to confession and had obtained absolution from the priest for their thoughts about what they intended to do. Talking to the priest seemed to have helped them. The job would now be a duty, not a pleasure, to them.

'I am glad,' I said. 'Now these are my orders: you must arrange the permanent disappearance of Dr Spiegel and his assistant. I might as well tell you that this decision is a joint decision by me and by our staff. The job will have to be carried out in silence and the corpses hidden as well as possible.'

Stas produced, apparently from nowhere, a hunting knife,

sharp as a razor, tapering to a needle-sharp point.

'This will do,' he said. 'As to when, we shall probably do it tomorrow near curfew. Spiegel will leave home after his evening meal to meet Peters.' We had expected that his assistant would be with him, but he had left Ostrowiec and would be dealt with later. Stas continued, 'We will hide the body in the thick reeds of the pool on the River Kamienna about a kilometre downstream of the bridge. It should stay there until the autumn rains.'

Next day I went to keep an eye on the proceedings. At about 7 pm Spiegel emerged from his house, flanked by Stas and another young man. All three were walking towards the river when a Field Gendarmerie patrol emerged from a side street. Fireworks will begin now, I thought. But nothing happened. Spiegel behaved quite normally and off they went. Ever since, I have wondered why it is that some people, knowing that they are going to certain death, do nothing about it? Some sort of hope against hope? Spiegel must surely have known where he was going, and yet he did not even try to attract the attention of the patrol. Why?

Two days later a freak rainstorm occurred and in a few hours the river was nearly bursting its banks. Next day Spiegel's body was found floating a few kilometres down the river. The discovery made the Gestapo furious. Everyone had to lie low for a few days because of the road blocks and the constant checking of documents. The food smugglers suffered most. Everything they carried was confiscated; people were harassed on the streets; spot checks were made on houses. I had taken home two hand grenades, my pistol and plenty of ammunition. Fortunately for me the house-to-house searches were confined to parts of the town where there were no regular army patrols and I could feel safe.

The flurry of German activity subsided after a week or so, when rumours started to circulate that people were taking bets on how long Spiegel's assistant would survive. Indeed, ten days later he was found on the road to Opatow, shot in the back of the head. By a freak accident, the bullet had not entered the brain, but, missing the spinal cord, had torn off his lower jaw and most of his tongue. He was taken to Ostrowiec, alive but unconscious, and placed in the hospital ward reserved for Germans. A uniformed Polish policeman was placed on guard at the door.

Two days later two young men in white hospital overalls entered the hospital. The Polish policeman was gagged and bound. The two men entered the ward and said in German that no harm would be done to any of the Germans provided everyone kept quiet. In the dead silence they approached the bed which held the unfortunate traitor, discussed briefly in German why the previous shot had gone wrong and then blew his brains out. Unmolested, they left the ward and the hospital.

There was, however, a German 'casualty'. An official from the town hall was in the same ward with a very severe bout of constipation. It later transpired that he was found semi-conscious with fright and, to the discomfort of the other patients in the ward, completely cured of his constipation!

There were a few other minor things I had to attend to. Two Polish families in Ostrowiec had been very friendly with the Germans. They had been warned by their acquaintances about their behaviour, but had rudely spurned the advice given them and carried on as if nothing had happened. I gave orders that the two heads of the families each be given fifteen strokes of the bullwhip. The bullwhip is a terrible instrument. It is made of the penis of a bull. When dried and twisted it is about a yard long, tough and very elastic. The first victim nearly died after fifteen strokes, so the second was given only ten.

These actions proved to be enough. The population's morale improved and the Germans became completely cut off from any unofficial contact with the people. Peters was fuming. Soldau was notified by post that he would have to be more restrained if he wanted to survive.

It was now June, 1941. For me this was a period of hectic

activity. The money from Dahlia was beginning to pour in in quite large amounts, so I obtained the consent of the Finance Committee to use some of it to buy a new bicycle and, through my old contacts, got a new machine from the bicycle factory in Radom. But I had to fetch it myself. The pass from Frank's office in Cracow was quite impressive, so I went by train to Radom and cycled back, using secondary roads. The bicycle, at last with good brakes, proved invaluable on my extensive travels throughout the District. I was able to appoint a reserve officer as the local C.O., south of the Holy Cross Mountains. He lived with a forester whom we will call Mr V., a wonderfully hospitable chap and a naturalized Czech. In the eastern area of the District, at Ozarow, I met a born leader, a young man named Witold, who had already organized about a hundred men and had a considerable amount of arms and ammunition. Witold's territory was suitable for air drops, which I hoped would eventually materialize. I was able to find, and to establish, many safe houses for myself and for anyone sent from Provincial Headquarters. Everywhere I went I had plenty to eat and the only problem I had was how to avoid excessive drinking. With everyone demonstrating their support and hospitality to the full, I had to use all my tact and diplomacy to cope with the problem. As well as my travels for the Organization, I also had to make several journeys in my capacity as the Sugar-Beet Inspector. I began to know my District inside out, its forests, tracks, villages and isolated houses. There were so many military police on the roads that travel was quite easy, the Gestapo and the Gendarmerie being confined to their own headquarters.

Then, at 3 am on 21 June a continuous, distant rumbling noise could be heard from the east. As expected, Germany had attacked Russia. During the months of May and June Drake had submitted reports nearly every day about the impending attack on Russia, reports compiled from many sources, military, civilian and Security. All these reports were sent by me to the Provincial Commander. I did not know whether or not the reports were sent to Warsaw and thence to England.

I could now foresee new problems. When the Germans had over-run Poland in 1939, the gates of the Holy Cross prison in the mountains had been opened. The prison was for prisoners convicted of murder and armed robbery. In September, 1939, they all escaped. Some of them disappeared altogether, but others stayed in the District, living by robbery and violence. Some had been liquidated, but the hard core, armed and ruthless, bedevilled the life of the populace.

I did not mind the professional thieves. Most of them were good Poles and patriots, exercising their skills on Germans. As a young officer I had myself had a batman who, when asked about his profession in civilian life, had answered quite frankly that he was a professional thief, as were his father and his grandfather, and that it was the only profession he knew. I was lucky to get him. During the year I had this chap as batman I never missed a penny. My only problem was that other batmen would frequently turn up, asking if by any chance I had seen a spare tin of shoe polish or a duster. As a matter of fact, during that year I did not have to buy a single tin of shoe polish.

Murderers and muggers were quite a different kettle of fish. I knew that, now Germany was fighting Russia, the Communists would become active. Not, however, that they would join the Resistance Movement to fight the common enemy. They would, I felt sure, pursue Stalin's policy of liquidating as many of the Polish intelligentsia as possible. This is what the Russians had tried to do in 1939, by the deportation to the slave labour camps of about two million Poles. Every Pole showing any kind of leadership or initiative was sent in cattle trucks to Siberia. When I myself was taken prisoner by the Russians in September, 1939, I was able to observe how the criminal and most primitive elements of the population had been given control of the villages and the towns. As in 1917, the thieves, the robbers, rapists and psychopaths constituted the bulk of the muscle available to the Communists. The pattern was sure to be repeated as soon as the Communists received new orders from Moscow.

I knew that I would now have to fight on two fronts. I also knew that I would be fighting a losing battle.

V

The Germans and the People of the District

THE DISTRICT WAS rather lucky as far as the German administrative personnel were concerned. After the disappearance of Spiegel and his henchman, the Gestapo trod rather warily. Its chief, Soldau, tried his best to contact me, in order, as he used to say to all and sundry, to come to some sort of arrangement to 'fight our common enemy'. Because of this he kept in check his butcher, Peters, who very seldom left Gestapo headquarters. The Gendarmerie stationed at Ostrowiec were also behaving, making only sporadic excursions into the countryside to check the delivery of levies, to catch smugglers and to protect the sugar and cattle transports. Owing to the efforts of Soldau's secretary, every move of the Gendarmerie, or Gestapo, was known to me and to my staff well in advance. I could travel freely throughout my command, although the number of anonymous letters about me, intercepted at the Post Office, had increased considerably since 21 June. My limp was mentioned in some of the letters, but no other details were ever given. I knew that I had to face the fact that my limping gait was known to virtually everybody and that to all intents and purposes I was already 'blown'.

The SD chief, Donat, was under the influence of his wife and kept a very low profile. The only thing he wanted was to go back to Hamburg and his teaching. His SD men were of the same frame of mind and together they were doing very well by selling on the German black market all the flour they were getting from Roman. They were, of course, blind to the fact that Roman's mill was going day and night, producing not only the official quantity of flour required for the rationing, but also whatever flour was wanted for the black market. It was big business.

Kreishauptmann Moczal was seldom seen, except in his office at the Opatow town hall and in the flat near by, where he lived quietly with his family.

The man responsible for the agriculture and forestry of the District, for supervising the delivery of food levies and the supply of artificial manure, cigarettes and clothing to the farmers, all accounted for against the produce raised—and delivered, was one Baron von Böninghausen. He spoke beautiful French, the language he used in dealing with the landowners. At one of the meetings he started his introductory speech about the levies by saying, 'Gentlemen, I know that you are contributing towards the upkeep of the Underground . . .'

Before he could go on, one of the landowners, a certain Mr. L., stood up and said in a loud voice, 'I can assure you, Herr Baron, that I have never contributed a penny towards any illicit organization.'

The Baron looked at him with disgust. 'Monsieur L., I am ashamed for you. You must be a proper bastard. Shut up. I do not want either to talk or to listen to you.' The Baron left the meeting, ostentatiously refusing to shake hands with Mr. L.

On the whole life in the District was not too bad. The neighbouring District of Starachowice, on the other hand, had as its *Kreislandwirt*, Herr von Olszewski, a Pole by origin and a true renegade who used extortion, the police and the Gendarmerie to ensure delivery of his quota of foodstuffs. Eventually he was liquidated by the Underground.

So life went on, with some parts of the District, especially

45

south of the Holy Cross mountains, not being visited by the Germans at all. Eventually this part of the country became known as the Rakow Republic. In the sixteenth century Rakow was the centre of the Arian movement, an enlightened Protestant group with political and social ideas far in advance of those prevailing in Poland at the time.

The Polish population could be divided into three main groups: the landowners and the gentry; the peasants; the workers, including some craftsmen living in the country. Let us discuss, first of all, the landowners. In the Opatow District the representatives of this class were quite different from my childhood notions of a landowner. I was born on the eastern border of pre-partition Poland. There, a landowner with one thousand acres, say, was considered to be a smallholder, with a way of life comparable to that of a well-to-do peasant. Although gentry by birth, they lived without any pretence to being better than those around them. Successive partitions, uprisings and rebellions against Russian domination had reduced their living standards to a primitive level. Large landowners in those eastern areas, on the other hand, had immense holdings. These extended from some forty thousand acres to whole provinces. Tsar Alexander III, for instance, when travelling by sleigh to Odessa, asked on four successive days across whose land he had been travelling. For four days the answer was: on the land of Count Potocki (this particular branch of the Potocki family had obtained the land from Catherine the Great for assisting in the partition of Poland). But apart from the truly rich, the average landowner led a patriarchal sort of life, taking good care of his workers. I remembered my two great-aunts, who lived on an estate near the junction of the River Prypet with the Dnieper. No wedding, no christening in the village could take place without their consent, or their active participation. During the Russian Revolution they were thrown out of their manor house by a special commission sent from Moscow. All their furniture, silver, etc. was taken by the villagers for safekeeping. During the Polish army's advance to the Ukraine in 1920 every stick of furniture, every chattel and piece of silver was returned to their house. The last news my family had of them was that they were both living with, and being taken care of by, the villagers.

In the District the picture was totally different. There were a few estates of about four thousand acres, but most were the size of a large farm, one thousand acres or less. However, before the war nearly all the landowners had been living on a grand scale, well beyond their means, with plenty of servants, grooms, carriages and so on. They were addressed by their servants and by the villagers as 'Excellencies', 'Ladyships', and the like. Nearly all of them considered themselves a cut above ordinary middle-class folk. When I became acquainted with them in my official capacity, I was quickly able to sum them up. I had no illusions. I could categorize them into a few distinct groups: brutes; gentlemen and gentlewomen in the Shavian sense; true gentlemen and gentlewomen, people with a Christian outlook on life, full of compassion and love towards mankind. From the point of view of patriotism, they could be divided again into several distinct categories: those who did not give a damn about the country, the Germans or the war, but cared only for their pockets, which, because of the war and all sorts of shady deals, they could at long last fill (fortunately these were very few); patriots by 'tradition'—the Opatow District had been prominent in the uprising of 1863, providing quite a few outstanding leaders at the time, and had suffered heavy losses among its partisans in skirmishes with the Russian army—patriotic because it gave them a feeling of being 'fashionable', as it were; those who joined or aided the Underground because that provided a thrill in their otherwise dull life under the German occupation; and true patriots, who considered it their duty to the country, and to mankind, to fight or to provide aid for those who fought. Typical representatives of this latter group were two families, one headed by Mr Morawski from Planta, the other by Mr Halpert-Scanderbeg from the forest estate of Jeleniec, north of Ostrowiec.

Mr Morawski belonged to a family distinguished for its diplomats and civil servants. One brother had been the Polish Ambassador to France before the war. Another, living at Planta at the time, was a senator. He was ejected from his estate in the province of Poznan, when Poznan was incorporated into the Third Reich. The Morawskis had thirteen children. Mrs Morawski was a beautiful woman, full of quiet resolve. Their house was packed with refugees of all kinds. Among them was the well-known writer Parandowski and his wife, Mr Smotrycki, sports editor of the main newspaper in Katowice in Upper Silesia, and several young men of various origins. My first contact with the family was made over breakfast. I felt like the President of the United States on New Year's Day, I had to shake so many hands. I had the opportunity to stay at Planta on several occasions, one visit lasting several weeks. Whenever I had to stay with 'traditional' or 'fashionable' patriots, I could always feel a more or less well-concealed anxiety regarding my presence. I could understand the feeling. After all, they were risking their lives having me on the premises. The tension was, however, so tiring that I never stayed longer than I had to in such a house. At Planta, there was no feeling of fear. The food was adequate but simple. For breakfast, for instance, there was barley coffee with milk, bread and turnips. Mr Morawski's attitude was that, having such a large family and being responsible for the well-being of so many people, he could not afford to indulge in rich meals. At the same time there was nothing he would not give for the needs of the Underground; his contributions were quite substantial. All in all, a wonderful family.

I became acquainted with the Halpert family through Dahlia. She insisted that I make Mr Halpert's acquaintance, and Mr Halpert was also eager to know me. Potentially he could be very useful in many respects. I met him at Dahlia's home. He told me that for some time now he had been in contact with Soldau, pestering the latter about protection against the so-called 'bandits'. His home, Jeleniec, was deep in the forest, within the operating range of these 'bands' (or so he told the Gestapo).

He did not, of course, get any protection from the Germans, but Soldau did present him with a brand new army rifle and a hundred rounds of ammunition.

Halpert asked for my approval of his fostering Soldau's attention and, having obtained it, invited me to come with him to spend a few days at Jeleniec. I agreed. He telephoned his wife to say that he would be coming home with a guest, and off we went.

I was wearing khaki breeches and riding boots and looked rather military. When we arrived at Jeleniec and entered the dining room, the time being about 6 pm, several people discreetly vanished and only Mrs Halpert came to greet me. She was an imposing lady, in evening dress with a large emerald at her throat. When I was introduced to her, she began to laugh. What had happened was that, on leaving home, Mr Halpert had said that he would go and see Soldau again about the protection scheme. When he rang up his wife, saying that he would be coming home with an unexpected guest, everyone assumed that it would be the Gestapo chief; this was why everybody had disappeared from the room when the unexpected guest arrived.

They were an amazing family. Mr Halpert was the heir to a banking fortune established by his great-grandfather, a Frankist, i.e. a Jew belonging to the Frankist movement who, late in the eighteenth century, had adopted the Christian faith. The hyphenated name of Scanderbeg was taken from his maternal grandfather, a Montenegrin chieftain who had found himself at the court of Tsar Alexander II of Russia.

Mr H. was a thick-set, jolly man, with a great paunch and a splendid sense of humour. He spoke perfect Russian, German, French and English. He was a graduate of the Agricultural Faculty of the University of Leipzig. For some time, in the late twenties, he had been Secretary of the Polish Embassy in

London. He was a great gourmet, had been on several safaris to Africa, was a wonderful shot and a superb host. Living somewhat beyond his quite considerable means, he eventually had to retire to Jeleniec, the forest estate which had belonged originally to his wife Maria, whose maiden name was Wielopolska, a well-known Polish family. Mrs Halpert's father had once owned nearly half the land in the District, including a huge sugar refinery and steel works. He lost very nearly all of this at baccarat one night in St Petersburg, and only Jeleniec was left, with its twelve thousand acres of forest and poor soil.

The old manor house had been extended to include several guest bedrooms and a two-storey hall, round which hung hunting trophies.

When I went there the house was full. There was Professor Wiechowicz of the Poznan Conservatoire, the Reverend Nowak from Poznan, the well-known violinist Eugenia Uminska, the wife and two daughters of the well-known pianist Zygmunt Dygat and, lastly, Mr and Mrs Polikier. Mr Polikier, a Jew, was a mathematics graduate from Göttingen who became one of the most successful solicitors in Warsaw. Their son, Joseph, was in hiding on one of the estates in the district.

Jeleniec was nearly all forest, with sandy soil and a few open patches on which potatoes and some buckwheat could grow. The household, apart from the guests, comprised two maids, a chef (who had very little to cook), a laundry woman and a few auxiliary staff. They all survived by the illicit sale of wood. This was obtained very cleverly, leaving no visible scars on the forest. Although the lady of the house always changed for dinner, the dinner itself consisted of one dish only, a vegetable soup with a few pieces of meat floating in it. This was definitely not enough for Mr Halpert. His appetite was tremendous, and after the evening meal, he used shame-facedly to devour meat sandwiches in his bedroom, out of sight of everyone else.

50

I stayed with them for a few days. An alibi had been arranged for me. I was supposed to be a distant relative from the east of Poland. All the details of the relationship had been meticulously worked out. The evening after my arrival Mr Halpert invited me to his bedroom after the evening meal and said, 'Now we shall have a proper meal. I suggest: broiled lobster with fresh melted butter, turbot à la Polonaise, steak Chateaubriand, pêche Melba, assorted cheeses, black coffee, brandy and a Havana to round the meal off. How about that?' Nice meal, thought I. Unfortunately it was only a thought.

In September, all being quiet in the District, I began to think about my wife and son. The time seemed ripe for all of us to be reunited. We had parted in February, 1940, when I escaped from the military hospital to try and join the Polish Navy, which was under British command and based in Great Britain. After the dreadful winter of 1939–40 in Warsaw, my wife took our son to live with a cousin of mine, a Ukrainian who had a smallholding near the village of Dwikozy on the south-east border of the District. My cousin's living conditions were poor; he eked out a meagre living by growing tomatoes and maize. For good measure he also kept a few cows and pigs; the cattle found grazing, albeit poor, in the ravines of this loess country, and his pigs and goats were of the variety which needed very little sustenance to survive, to breed and to provide some meat and milk.

The house they all lived in was very old, damp and cold. Besides my cousin there was his wife, their only child, a boy, his mother-in-law (the widow of a university professor, a dragon of a woman), and two cousins, one on his mother's and the other on his father's side, the latter with his wife. The first of the cousins, an officer of the old Imperial Guard, drank heavily; the other was an unbelievably cowardly man.

At the outbreak of war between Germany and Russia, the Ukrainians, who were always very anti-Russian, welcomed the German Army as a liberating force and immediately the Germans formed a Ukrainian SS Division and began to single out the Ukrainians left within the borders of Poland for favours. Since my cousin was a Ukrainian, the Gestapo started to visit him quite often, trying to woo him to their side, but without result. He was at peace with everyone and wanted to remain so. These visits, and his amicable relations with the Gestapo and Gendarmerie, made his home a very 'safe house', and Irena, my wife, felt quite secure living with him. Her life was not, however, easy, mainly because of the proverbial problem of the presence of the mother-in-law. Moreover, both Irena and I felt frustrated living apart. I decided, therefore, to arrange for my family to leave my cousin and come to live somewhere nearer to me, somewhere in my District.

Dahlia understood my problem and offered me and my family room and board at her home. In November, 1941, Roman sent a cart with a pair of horses to fetch Irena and Andrew and take them to their new home. I could now visit them as often as possible and I could even stay with them whenever I could. Another problem seemed resolved, though for how long neither I nor anybody else could tell.

But another problem arose which had to be resolved. While I was on the staff of the Provincial Headquarters in Kielce, a 'blown' colonel arrived from Cracow. A very conspicuous man, very tall, with a prominent duck's bill of a nose, he had been commanding officer before and during the war of a border regiment consisting mainly of conscript Ukrainians. He was put in my care because as a conspirator he was an innocent. He had virtually no initiative, and I had to look after him, provide him and his wife with lodgings, arrange for safe places for him to eat at and to meet other people, show him the routes to be taken from one meeting place to another, and so on. His position on the Provincial Staff was not at all clear. The powers-that-be decided, therefore, in November, 1941, that he be appointed as Inspector of the Organization for the District of Opatow and the neighbouring one of Sandomierz—pure bureaucracy, which was bound to complicate communications between the Province and the High

Command in Warsaw, with which I sometimes had to deal directly.

As I have mentioned, I had to find him and his wife a safe house and to provide them with all the necessary amenities of life. One of the amenities the Inspector required was plenty of drink, as well as plenty to eat. Extra meetings had to be held for the Inspector and the District Staff, which involved providing the Inspector with transport. I had to take him round my territory to familiarize him with the terrain and the people. The Inspector adopted the pseudonym of Tench (*Lin* in Polish). His true name was Zolkiewski, the name of the famous Polish military leader of the sixteenth century. Because my superior has chosen a fishy *nom de guerre*, I decided to change mine to a fishy name as well. I chose Grayling, and that became the name under which I was known until 1945.

Patriots by tradition and patriots by fashion made up the majority of the landowners in the district. Actually it was difficult to differentiate between the two. What one might have said about the 'patriots by tradition' was that they felt obliged to be patriotic, out of a sense of duty rather than a genuine emotion. Thus, feeling compelled to be patriots, they felt that they were among the hard core of the fighting people. To talk to them, let alone to stay with them, was a mental and moral ordeal. One could feel their insincerity and their underlying anxiety about being seen talking to me, or doing something for the Underground. One could hear the audible sigh of relief when I left. The fashionables were engaged in Underground activities of one sort or another for the thrill of it. Sooner or later the stress would prove too much; a breaking point came; suddenly they were deadly afraid, often without any real reason, and that was that.

The peasants were a different matter, in strong contrast to the landowners. After a few months of meeting their representatives, who spoke for eighty-five per cent of the population, I began to feel true respect for them. I realized that these people constituted the real strength of the nation. Nearly all of them

53

were wise, cagey and distrustful of strangers. All had a deep-rooted feeling of 'belonging'. This feeling arose from a deep attachment to the soil they cultivated. In defending their right to the soil they showed themselves to be true patriots, without even knowing the meaning of the word. The District was in the centre of Poland and, apart from a small injection of Italian blood through the architects and masons who, in the sixteenth century, worked on the huge castle of Ossolin (destroyed during the Swedish–Polish wars of the seventeenth century), they were of pure Polish stock, going back to the beginning of Polish history. Throughout the centuries they had been neglected and abused by the gentry. Now, I thought, with the intelligentsia being slaughtered both by the Germans and the Russians, they would become the mainstay of the national revival. They would have to provide the source for the nation's intellectual and technological potential.

Before the war there existed an official People's Party, much too far to the left for the liking of the ruling régime. Now that party was, of course, Underground. Unfortunately, its active part was made up of badly organized peasants' battalions. Efforts were being made by the High Command to incorporate these battalions into the Home Army. They were, however, still apprehensive of the Colonels' régime and, though loyal, were rather reluctant to be officially subordinated to the Government-in-exile. Since they were generally inactive, their presence, indeed their very existence, was not significant in the District.

The last group, the workers, nearly all belonged to the old Polish Socialist Party, a party with a long tradition of violence and sabotage directed against the occupying powers. Actually it would be wrong to speak of the Socialist Party as a workers' party only. It used to comprise many of the intelligentsia as well. For instance, most of my staff were members of this Party, including S. and Blackie. In the District the Socialists were all very loosely organized along pre-war Party lines. Without much fuss they had organized the sabotaging of the

54

German war effort at places where they could do it by virtue of their occupation. The steel mill at Ostrowiec had the task of producing conning-towers for German long-range submarines. By craftily altering the vital dimensions on the drawings, the conning-towers produced at Ostrowiec were a poor fit or no fit at all when assembled with the hulls. The assembly took place elsewhere, inside the Reich. The alterations were made so cunningly that, although several investigating teams were sent to find the reasons, they could not discover where the alterations were being made or how. Nothing could be proved, so the blame was laid on the inefficiency of the Polish worker, and the production of conning-towers in Ostrowiec had to be abandoned early in 1942.

It was a pleasure to see these people working and to hear them talking. Love of Country was as deep as it was unobtrusive. Afraid or not, they were always ready to help and to advise.

Craftsmen were difficult to find. They had to lie low in order to avoid being deported to Germany as skilled labour. Owing to the concerted efforts of my staff, enough of them were spirited away from their jobs to establish a very efficient hand-grenade assembly workshop and an arms repair and reconditioning unit.

And so the year 1942 started to shape up very well indeed. The District was as quiet as could be expected. Funds were flowing in in increasing amounts and I was able to notify the Provincial C.O. that I would not require any subsidies, apart from my own salary. When I presented my budget which was quite substantial, I immediately received an order to divert part of our funds to Provincial Headquarters. I had great satisfaction in telling my superior that I personally had nothing to do with raising these funds, that the distribution and the budgeting were in the hands of a special committee and that I would have to submit to his committee the idea of transferring funds to Headquarters. Dahlia and the committee did not agree and Headquarters had to abandon their request.

My idea of purchasing, if necessary, the arms hidden throughout the countryside was beginning to produce very good results. Hundreds of rifles, boxes of ammunition, machine-guns, anti-tank rifles and even two anti-tank guns, had been recovered, cleaned, repaired and made ready for use. There was, however, a problem. The Post Office had begun to intercept more and more anonymous letters about me to the Gestapo and the police. No precise details were given, but they contained strong hints about somebody travelling around the countryside organizing the Resistance forces. I had to be more careful in my travels, changing my means of transport all the time—from bicycle to horseback, back to the bicycle, then to a horse-drawn cab, and so on. I also had to have all the information, every day, about the probable movements of the Gendarmerie and the SD patrols. It involved more meetings with the messengers, or rather with Maria. I was lucky, however, always to have the necessary information and I could move around the District relatively safely, although I was shown by Drake the first edition of the Gestapo *Fahnungsblatt*, where I found my proper name marked: 'Wanted for armed robbery. Dangerous.'

When starting on a journey I used to take out of its hiding place my Wis, the Polish Army regulation pistol, the most beautifully balanced, the most accurate and easy to use that I knew. Only once did I have to put it to use.

One day, on an empty track I was driving along peacefully behind my mare, minding my own business, when suddenly two men sprang on to the road from behind some bushes. One of them grabbed the mare by her halter and the other man approached me and demanded money, threatening me with a knife.

'I have no money on me', I answered.

'Don't give me that', said the man. 'You are decently clothed and have a horse. Don't tell me you have no money. Hand it over or else.'

56

'What else? Would you kill me?'

'We won't kill you, but if you don't hand over the money we will beat you up and take it by force.'

'Do you mean it?'

'Of course we do. Come on.' He reached out to grab my lapel.

'All right, all right,' I said. 'There is no need for violence.' I reached into my pocket and produced my Wis. I cocked it and said, 'Sit down by the bush at the side of the road.'

They sat, open-mouthed, eyes bulging. Robbery was a difficult problem. Some robbers were professionals, the remnants of the criminal élite, as it were, released from the Holy Cross prison. I had to make up my mind. I looked at them. Both wore shabby clothes, both were emaciated and both looked hungry.

'Why do you do it?' I asked.

'We have to, Governor. We have no jobs and we have been hungry since the war started.'

'Did you not have a job?'

'Oh yes, we did. We were in a navvy outfit maintaining the road between Radom and Kielce. But now this is the road used by the b . . . Germans and we do not want to help them in any way.'

'You could still get a job on a farm, or in a factory, or with some Polish firm.'

'Seeing that you carry a gun, Guv, we'll be frank with you. We are professional thieves. We were quite successful before the war, but now, how could we steal with so much misery and poverty around? We have never carried arms; we have never harmed anybody. We thought to stay in the army after having done our national service, but then, you see, we don't know how to write or even read, so they did not want us in the army either.'

'All very well,' I said, 'but you have threatened me with a knife and have promised to carve me up if I don't produce the money.'

57

'Eeh, that's only talk. We try to pick on people who look as if they could spare a few zlotys. We only take as much as we need for some food and to pay the rent this blasted woman charges us for the shack we live in. Have a heart, Guv, and let us go. We didn't mean any harm, really we didn't.'

I looked at them for a long time. A small voice was telling me that the two men were all right. I made up my mind. Putting my pistol back into my pocket, I said, 'All right. I'll let you go. But leading this sort of life, you'll be caught sooner or later and then it's the concentration camp and curtains for you. Go home now, and if you give me your address somebody will come and see you. One more thing: you will forget about meeting me. If you talk to anyone I shall know and you will be sorry. Go in peace now. Perhaps we shall see each other again. Here are a few zlotys to tide you over.'

They did not know quite what to say. They looked with unbelieving eyes at the money and then at me. They, too, were probably making up their minds.

'I've not got much of it myself,' I said. 'I don't rob people. Go in peace.' I touched the reins and left them staring after me.

The next day, when I saw Drake, I suggested that he check out the two men as soon as possible. If they were genuine, Drake could use them in his outfit; if not, then Stas would have another job. (They turned out all right. They joined Stas's team and proved to be an asset in the Organization.)

By this time I felt completely at home wherever I went. I knew every road, every path, every village. I had four safe houses at Ostrowiec, one at Jeleniec, four east of Ostrowiec and four south of it. I had four safe houses at or near Opatow, three on the road leading west and two between Ostrowiec and Opatow. Wherever I stayed the night I was always well fed. As to sleeping accommodation, it varied from a proper bed to a barn with hay or straw. One thing which sometimes bothered me were lice. I did not mind fleas; I could stand any number of them. One louse, however, set me itching all over, and one night, when I was in bed, I saw on the edge of the

58

blanket, a mother louse and a dozen or so smaller lice crawling behind her. I had to get up and go to sleep in the barn.

I was able to lodge the Inspector and his wife on one of the estates. Initially he went everywhere with me, using the bicycle I had provided. After a while, however, he found this method of transport too exhausting and always tried to scrounge a horse-drawn carriage from someone. It was not easy and was rather conspicuous, so I had to try to avoid accompanying him. We used to arrive at the rendezvous separately.

VI

The Wylag Affair

To say that the District was relatively quiet is a figure of speech. The quiet was indeed relative. Every day young men were forcibly seized and deported as slave labour to the Reich, or forced into the Todt Organization which operated all over Europe. More to the point, since the disposal of Spiegel and his henchman, the Gestapo began to make sporadic individual arrests, mainly among the refugees from the Poznan region, which had been incorporated into the Reich. There was never a warning. Men and women, sometimes whole families, were arrested without any apparent pattern. For a few days or weeks they were detained by the Gestapo; then they just disappeared. It became quite a normal procedure. People lived in the constant expectation of arbitrary arrest at any time.

One day the whole Wylag family was arrested. The father had been a town clerk somewhere in Poznanie. At the outbreak of the war his eldest son was just old enough to be drafted into the army; as an ordinary soldier he was released by the Germans and allowed to go home. They were all deported to the General Gouvernement in December, 1939. Now, after three weeks of being held at Gestapo Headquarters, the family was suddenly released. It looked suspicious and Drake kept a very close check on the family at all times.

In April, 1942, I was still officially working at the seed merchant's. One of the employees there was the young

Wylag. His father had found work as an inspector of cattle and pig tagging on behalf of the *Kreislandwirt*.

I was informed that young Wylag had begun to ask questions about me, making remarks such as, 'This chap working with us does not seem to fit very well into his job; he is away a lot; his reports about the sugar beet seed plantations are rather casual; etc, etc.'

Drake already knew that both father and son had been coerced into the service of the Gestapo. At least twice a week they could both be seen leaving Gestapo Headquarters, where they had gone to practise pistol shooting. Both were known to carry guns. Young Wylag did not seem to be immediately dangerous. His father, on the other hand, appeared to be doing a lot of harm. As an official checking the tagging of cattle and pigs he visited every village and household in the District. People were already complaining that he was blackmailing farmers and smallholders into paying him large amounts of money whenever he found an untagged animal. People paid up because to be reported usually meant the concentration camp, if not an outright execution. Yet people who were known to have paid blackmail money were being arrested. A number of villages had been searched, which showed that the Germans suspected the existence of hidden arms. It was quite clear that only Wylag could have supplied the Germans with information about the possibility of arms being hidden at such and such a place. After all, people talk, especially after a few glasses of moonshine vodka. They are also proud of, and like to boast about, their achievements or about what they have.

Drake asked for permission to liquidate both of them. This presented me with a dilemma. After all, I was not as yet troubled by the Gestapo, as no surveillance could be observed. If I gave the order to dispose of young Wylag, people could say that I did it to protect myself, that I was afraid of a youngster. I refused to give the order, but at the same time gave notice and officially quit my employment, saying that I was leaving Ostrowiec. And this I did.

Old Wylag was a different proposition. Too many Gendarmerie patrols were going into the countryside in his wake. I told the execution squad to be ready.

A week later Drake learned from young Wylag that his father was supposed to come back to Ostrowiec from his tour of inspection by a particular pass through the Holy Cross Mountains, one which could easily take a horsedrawn cart. I ordered Stas and his team to lie in ambush at the top of the pass where the road was very narrow, and to wait for me without showing themselves until ordered by me to do otherwise.

I took a horse, a four-wheeler and my Wis and went off early in the morning to the pass from the other side of the mountains. I stopped at the narrowest part of the road and waited. Behind the bushes at the side of the road I could see Stas and his companions.

There was no traffic. The spruce forest, immortalized in Polish literature, was quiet, its tall trees reaching high into the sky, their branches forming a canopy over the road. Although it was a fine day, the road was enveloped in twilight, with only a few rays of sun breaking through the branches.

I waited for a long time. It was nearly noon when I first heard, then saw, Wylag approaching. He was singing and looked quite drunk.

'Hey, you over there,' he shouted. 'What's the idea of blocking the road? I am on official business, so move over and let me pass.'

I looked at him. I saw a middle-aged man with a face like a ferret and bloodshot eyes. He was wearing an expensive gaberdine overcoat, a felt hat and chamois leather gloves. He exuded confidence and even arrogance.

'I am sorry,' I said, 'but my horse is all in because of these mountain roads. But if you want to know, I am also on official business. I am the Sugar Beet Seed Inspector. Who are you?'

'I am Mr Wylag, the Cattle and Pig Tagging Inspector and I work for Baron von Böninghausen, if you want to know. So you are the chap who works for the same firm as my son. From what I have heard, you are not doing very well in your position.'

'How could one do well?' I said. 'A lot of travel, come fine weather or foul. The beet seed growers do not seem to appreciate the necessity of separating the sugar beet from the fodder beet. All sorts of false information is fed into the official reports and statistics. I am fed up with my work. On top of all this I realize that I'm serving the Germans, not our people.'

'Well, there is no need to be despondent. Here, come over to my cart and we shall have a frank talk and a glass of vodka. I have also some bread and sausage. Come on,' said Wylag.

I went over and sat beside him. We drank a glass of vodka and Wylag cut a generous slice of sausage and started to talk. He was at the stage of tipsiness when one is very voluble and likes to listen to one's own voice.

'You see, my dear man,' he said condescendingly, 'it all depends on one's attitude towards the realities of life. All right, I work for the Germans. You agree that they are the winners. One should always go with the winners. I have to snoop around villages and houses to see that every cow and every pig is tagged. You cannot imagine where I find un-tagged cattle. It is quite a tiring job, but it is very rewarding.'

'How?'

'Well, live and let live is my motto,' said Wylag. 'I am a reasonable man and we usually come to an agreement. They have so much money nowadays that a few zlotys here and a few zlotys there, spent wisely, does them no harm and keeps me quite well off.'

He reached into his breast pocket and brought out a wallet bulging with money. He opened it and I could see that the 'few zlotys here and a few zlotys there' amounted to quite a sum.

'I wish I had opportunities like you,' I said.

'Of course you have. The owners of the beet seed plan-tations would not like to have their crop classified as fodder, would they? There you are—a hint, a bit of pressure, and you are in clover. This is my method and you can see the results: plenty of money, good clothes, first-class travel if I want to relax. Why don't you try doing the same?'

'It is not the same with me. First of all, estates all over the country are having a hard time. Many owners have been arrested; many did not return from the war. Often those that remain are exploited by their stewards. How could I ask them to pay for withholding information from the Germans? It could also be dangerous for me.'

'Don't you believe in their difficulties. They are rolling in money. After all, they contribute generously towards the upkeep of the Underground, don't they?'

'Oh yes,' I said, 'I know many owners of estates who do so quite willingly.'

'Can you give me some names?' asked Wylag eagerly.

'Well, I don't know if it would be right. It could endanger their lives.'

'Of course you can give me the names. I tell you what, you give me the names and I shall make you my partner in the new money-making scheme I've just thought of.'

'How much could we get?'

'Oh ho, ho. Give me the names, and we shall be really rich. If I can have tens of thousands from the blasted peasants, imagine the money we could get from the really rich when we mention that we know about their participation in the Underground movement!'

'But that would be blackmail,' I said. 'If someone refuses to meet our demands, we would have to leak his name to the Germans and that would mean curtains for him.'

'In war, what do one or two more victims matter? I had to do this a few times on my own and believe me, there is nothing to it. People are, by now, used to disappearances and nobody seems to care anymore if a few more vanish.'

'Except their families.'

'They will be glad to inherit. One's own survival matters;

64

bugger everyone else's.' He took another drink and ate some more sausage.

'I don't know,' I said. 'It's true that I know many instances of people cooperating with the Underground, but I would be afraid to travel around the countryside with so much money in my pocket.'

'Here again I could be of some help,' said Wylag. 'Look at that.' He opened his overcoat and there was a shining Parabellum.

'Aren't you afraid that I will report you and your pistol to the Germans?'

'Why should I be afraid? They supplied me with it themselves, for my protection.'

'I did not know that your job was rated as dangerous by the Germans. It is the first time that I have seen a Pole armed by the Germans. Of course, I know of many who have arms, but, believe me, they were not supplied by the Germans.'

'There you are again,' said Wylag. 'That information, too, could be very useful and profitable. There is another way of making money, and getting various privileges which make life much easier. If you give me your address I will contact you in a few days and we shall discuss the matter further. All right?'

I gave him my address and promised to wait for him at home a few days later.

We said goodbye. As Wylag gathered up the reins, I said, 'There is another matter I would like to settle with you. Hand me over your wallet and your notebook. I would advise you not to resist my request.' I gave the prearranged signal and Stas, with his two friends, appeared behind Wylag.

'Why should I give it to you?' he asked.

'Because I am the Commanding Officer of the District Home Army and I am investigating allegations that you are a traitor and an agent of the Gestapo. Hand it over. And no funny business.'

Wylag began to tremble. His fingers were numb and Stas

had to help him unbutton his overcoat. Stas took Wylag's pistol and handed me the fat wallet and a notebook. The notebook proved to be a mine of all possible types of information: names of people who were probably members of the Underground, or who might possibly have caches of arms or ammunition. Lastly, the stupid man had a list of names with sums of money entered against them. I started to read these names and suddenly stopped.

'Wait a moment,' I said. 'You have entered here two names with large sums of money against them. But these two men have been arrested and have probably been sent to the concentration camp. In other words, you have extorted the blackmail money from them and then you have denounced them to the Gendarmerie. What do you say to that?'

He could not say anything. He continued to tremble. I looked at my two men. Both of them pointed their thumbs down.

'Mr Wylag,' I said, 'after seeing your notebook, and considering what you have said to me during our conversation, I have no doubt whatever that you are a traitor to your country and to humanity. You have to die. The execution will be carried out forthwith.'

Before we could do anything, a terrible stench arose from his trousers. He had defecated. Then he threw up a mass of undigested sausage, turned up his eyes and slumped in his seat in a dead faint.

I preferred it to be this way. We trussed him up to a tree, put a noose around his neck and let the horse move away. The rope was just too high for his legs to reach the ground. He hung, twisting slowly on the noose. Stas put a shot through his heart and we went away, leaving the corpse hanging over the road.

Wylag's corpse was discovered, or rather reported, two days later. His demise produced quite a stir at Gestapo and SD Headquarters, although in private Donat was congratulating Roman. Gendarmerie patrols were increased and Donat was

66

kept very busy going around Opatow and the neighbouring villages looking for clues. No arrests followed, but three days later the young Wylag was posted to a 'clerical' job in the neighbouring town of Sandomierz. Soldau had also probably decided that Peters had outlived his utility at Ostrowiec. Everyone knew him by sight and everything about him. According to Soldau's secretary, Peters was being posted far away, to Salonica in Greece.

It so happened at the time that a representative of the Todt Organization was at Ostrowiec, trying to recruit 'voluntary' labour for work on fortifications in various parts of Europe. News leaked that now he was actually recruiting for jobs in Greece. Perhaps that was the reason why Peters was being sent there, to keep an eye on young people he might remember from Ostrowiec.

A week or so after the death of Old Wylag, two young men approached Drake with the suggestion that they enlist for work in Greece and there take care of Peters. Peters had been instrumental in the arrest of quite a few members of their respective families.

Although there was an element of a private vendetta in this suggestion, I agreed. The two men enlisted and went off in a large group of men who had been seized by force.

It was a long shot, but it paid off. Three months later the Gestapo secretary informed Drake that Soldau was very upset: he had just had news that Peters had been shot dead by Greek bandits in a café in Salonica.

In August word came from the C.O. of Sandomierz with alarming news that young Wylag, notwithstanding all the warnings about him, had been able to penetrate the lower echelons of the Sandomierz Underground in a relatively short time. Already twenty people had been arrested and many more would follow in the near future if nothing were done about the informer. The Sandomierz C.O. was urgently requesting that Opatow arrange to liquidate Wylag—Sandomierz at that time had no execution squad. Black, the

Sandomierz C.O., suggested that Wylag be taken care of during one of the visits to the Ostrowiec Gestapo which he made every week. During his next visit he would probably be able to supply new names to Soldau, so time was running short.

With a feeling of relief, I issued the necessary orders. Wylag was to be killed before reaching the Gestapo Headquarters and watch had to be kept to intercept him on the outskirts of the town.

The next day young Wylag was met at the crossroads by one of his schoolmates from Poznan. After hearty greetings, Wylag's young friend sat down beside him and, still talking, shot him twice under the shoulderblade. Wylag died instantly.

The summer of 1942 was by now in full swing. There were no Wylags any more. I knew by then that I had been 'blown' hundreds of times over and that only my watchfulness and God's care would prevent my death. I could not afford to be taken alive, ever.

VII

The Communist and
the Russian Threat

THERE WERE STILL a few groups of bandits left in the District. Some had moved away, some had been liquidated by the police, some on my order. Since the German invasion of Russia, those who were left had been gradually taken over by the communists. I was quite right in my prediction: the communist groups, though rather small and badly armed, were being reinforced by those elements wanting more action, elements which lacked discipline and were anti-social, in that they were concerned only about themselves. They were not necessarily communist orientated; they joined the communists because the communists were promising everything and asking, for the time being, for virtually nothing. The Communist Party was always small in Poland and was always totally subservient to Russia. After June, 1941, the communists went deep underground. Their main centre for the Western Region was at Ludwikow, a suburb of Ostrowiec. Very often I was asked by members of my staff to break it up. I was in a quandary. What a situation! All my instincts told me that communism is a mortal enemy of the nation and of all it stands for. Now communists and the Communist Party were officially part of the Great Alliance—Russia was the Great Ally! Yet I knew that this alliance could not last for long. The break-up of some of the communist cells would result in some delay to their final victory, but delay only. Moreover, either we are a democratic nation, I thought, or we are not. Therefore, both for practical and political reasons, I ordered that the cell and Mr Gomulka, who used to visit it, were to be left well and truly alone.

By mid-summer, 1942, Russian parachutists were being air-lifted into Poland in large numbers. One of them, Sashka, who claimed to be a Ukrainian of Polish descent, had been infiltrated into the District. He was a man of great courage and initiative. He started to take over command of all those communist groupings led until now by the criminal elements. It became clear to me that sooner or later these groups would become the kernel of the so called 'People's Guard', a military organization by now well-publicized by Moscow Radio. Officially they were the armed section of the Polish Communist Party.

Sashka clearly had no funds and robberies around the countryside started to be carried out on a grand scale, adding another burden on the people.

It became impossible to deal with these groups without an effective field force and, against Tench's judgement, I asked the High Command of the Home Army in Warsaw, through the intermediary of the Provincial C.O., for permission to form, and to put into the field, a small force of, say, fifty men, which could maintain a high profile in the countryside and could deal efficiently with these groups of bandits. Permission, however, was flatly refused, although it was widely known that field forces were in fact operating on behalf of the High Command. In November a partisan detachment of the Home Army forces, under the leadership of Lieutenant Ponury (Piwny) appeared in the region of the Holy Cross Mountains, retreating from the west after heavy fighting with the Germans. There were about a hundred men, very well armed, but without winter clothing and without any food supplies. They were probably the reason why the High Command had refused permission for me to form my own partisan group. I had been informed that Ponury had received

70

orders to cooperate fully with me and I had been ordered to give him any help he would need. Ponury was, however, a 'big' man, reluctant to cooperate and anxious to find excuses for his shortcomings.

He posed a new problem. The people had to cope, not only with the possibility of reprisals (I vividly remembered the case in 1940 of the celebrated Major Hubala who refused to lay down his arms, made himself the commanding officer of one hundred or so men and started to show off in the region of Wloszczowa. Ultimately his action resulted not only in his own death but, much more serious, in the death of two thousand inhabitants of two villages) but, whether they wanted it or not, they had to supply food and shelter to a group of men about whom they knew nothing.

I got news of Ponury soon after he arrived. Somehow a modus vivendi had to be found. Tench expressed a wish to meet him, but too many people would see Tench if he went to meet Ponury himself, and he did not want Ponury to come and see him. Such a visit would 'blow' his residence. Since no other way of meeting Ponury could be found, Tench abandoned the idea of seeing him and I was left to approach him on my own and to discuss with him all the problems resulting from the partisans' presence. So I went to see Ponury, camping deep in the larch forest on the northern slopes of the Holy Cross Mountains.

He had been parachuted from England a few weeks earlier. His men were from various regions of Poland, come together in haphazard fashion. His second-in-command was Lieutenant Nurt (Kaszynski); his adjutant was Lieutenant A. They had no clearly defined task. The High Command was also in a quandary. On one hand, since the Stalin-Sikorski pact, the Home Army was officially recognized as engaged in fighting the common enemy, the Germans. On the other hand, there was no doubt as to the intentions of the Russians. Katyn had already been discovered. Only a fraction of the Poles deported in 1939–1940 were allowed to join the Polish

71

Army being formed by General Anders in Russia. I had orders to carry out sabotage where possible, but not on supplies running from west to east to the front. Unofficially, sabotage was permitted only along the railwaylines running north–south. This was Ponury's task. When superior German forces attacked him, he was to withdraw through the dense forest into the Holy Cross Mountains, to rest and take care of his wounded.

Another independent group of saboteurs appeared in the south, in the region of the so-called Rakow Republic, a region into which Germans seldom ventured. They were led by Andy (Jedrus) and they were hindering the German war effort by snatching the sugar refined in the region and transported by narrow gauge railway to Sandomierz. They had already staged a spectacular prison break-out at Mielec. Their chief executioner, Walter, and his helper, Bobo, were keeping the region clear of informers and German agents.

Andy's group were quite intransigent and did not want to submit to any authority. Their behaviour was, however, without reproach and they did not present any danger to the populace.

Another small group under the leadership of one Tarzan, a sergeant-major, began to operate in the east.

The presence of these more or less independent groups was bound to lead, sooner or later, to conflict with the communist-led bands. Sashka had difficulty in binding these groups together. During the second half of 1942 several of these communist-led groups were caught and dispersed. Every such mishap was thought by them (and quite rightly) to be instigated by me and I soon learned that every one of these groups was looking forward to the time when they could find and dispose of the 'Lame Devil', as they called me.

In November, 1942, the first blow hit me and my Staff. During a random check in the streets of Ostrowiec, Maria was arrested. The Home Army news sheet, the *News*, had been found on her.

72

Unaware of her arrest, I went to Ostrowiec and could not find any of my Staff. Everyone had gone into hiding. I could make no contact with anyone. My landlady mentioned the arrest 'of this nice young girl Maria'. I had to do something about the situation. I assumed, rightly as it turned out, that Maria would keep her mouth shut. After all she would only have to answer questions about the news sheet. I was also pretty sure that many people knew what I looked like. First of all, therefore, I armed myself and somewhat ostentatiously bicycled several times through the streets before going to my 'safe' house, of which Maria, of course, knew the address. I had to wait for three days. On the third day a girl came from S. with the news that the Staff would be waiting for me at S.'s house.

They were somewhat ashamed of their panic. The news from the Gestapo's secretary was that Maria's beating had stopped and that it seemed that she had managed to convince Soldau that she obtained the *News* from a girl from Warsaw, whom she did not know. She was to be transported to Oswiecim (Auschwitz) without further interrogation. So that was that. By the time Ponury had been contacted and asked to spring her, Maria was already on her way to the concentration camp. Life returned to normal.

Another officer, blown in Lublin, joined the District Staff as combat instructor. He was a regular-army captain, using as a pseudonym Dionysius (Dyzio), who used his feet as a means of transport and could move unobtrusively and very quickly from place to place.

I could now go and join my wife and son again. But Dahlia was cracking. One morning she asked me to come and see her. She was in bed and by just looking at her I knew what was to come. She was sweating profusely and, in a broken and halting voice, she told me that she could not stand it any more and had to ask me and my wife to leave. Our son, Andrew, could stay with her and she would take care of him.

I thanked her for her hospitality. We agreed on the means

73

of communicating with each other and off my wife and I went.

By this time I had asked for and obtained permission from the finance committee to buy a horse. Witold got it for me. It was a mare, about 15 hands, compact, strong and very intelligent. After a few weeks she knew the meaning of the words 'turn left' or 'turn right'. At every crossroads she used to stop and look enquiringly at me to learn where to go. She was completely docile but had a sort of inhibition about her tail being shifted to the side. When harnessing her, I had to have quite a talk with her, telling her that I was not a stallion and that I did not intend to mount her. After a while she stopped being awkward and I could finish the harnessing without any trouble. She must have had some sort of hysterical feeling about stallions, because when in heat and taken to a stud farm, she nearly brought the barn down when she felt the approach of the stallion. She resisted so fiercely that she could not be mounted and I had to abandon the idea of having a foal from her.

I left a sealed envelope with Dahlia which contained our family name and my signet ring, just in case. Since leaving Dahlia, both my wife and I had been moving from house to house together. My wife was now acting as my messenger.

The communists by then were after me in full cry. We had to move from one place to another every few weeks. A few times the communists missed me or my wife by only a few hours, sometimes by less. My wife had orders to be ready to move at any moment, day or night.

This continuous odyssey enabled me to get to know, to respect and to love those very many people who were risking their lives to give us shelter. They usually did it in the most natural and informal manner. For example, I recall a certain Mr B. from the village of Milejowice. Mr B. was uncouth and rough, about sixty years of age. He was a typical Pole; his wife must have had some Italian blood, for their four sons were tall and blond. Mr B. had no table manners to speak of. He used to

74

spit on to the floor and to wipe his nose with his fingers. With all this he was a gentleman in the true sense of the word: sensitive to the feelings of other people, gentle and sincere. When he was giving he did it in a way that made it easy for others to accept. No heroics, no ego could be detected in his behaviour. He farmed his two hundred acres at the foot of the Holy Cross Mountains as his ancestors had for generations. One evening, while talking to me, he went to an old oak chest and took from it a rolled parchment and gave it to me. I looked at it with awe: it was the deed for Mr B.'s land, given to his ancestor by a Polish King of the thirteenth century, signed by the King and bearing the great seal of the Realm! Mr B. belonged. Such men were, and, I thought, will be, the backbone of the Nation.

In March, 1943, an order came from the High Command of the Home Army in Warsaw to initiate Action 'Swill', meaning the liquidation of all the existing banditry in the country. I sent back a memo stating that the action had been initiated too late; that by then all the bands were already under the aegis of either the Communist Party or the Russians themselves. Any possibility of getting rid of the bandits had been lost nearly a year before when I was refused permission to set up an independent field force able to deal with this problem. Now, I said, any attempt to get rid of these people would be interpreted as a hostile political action towards the Russians, incompatible with the accepted attitude of the Polish Government towards Russia. The answer came back from Warsaw: 'politics is not your problem; execute the order given.'

As usual, I thought, the bigger the organization the more remote it is from the real issues and the grass roots.

Tench summoned me to discuss the execution of 'Swill'. He must have been thoroughly briefed by the Provincial C.O. because he did not listen to any of my objections, but wanted the action to be carried out his way.

As the basis of the operation he made a theoretical military assumption that the total disruption of enemy communica-

75

tions must lead to the dispersion and then to the destruction of enemy forces. In vain I tried to point out that this theoretical approach would be ineffective, if not disastrous. No means of communication, in its standard military sense, existed between the groups which had to be destroyed. I tried to make Tench understand that all communications in any underground movement were carried out by individuals, moving from one location to another, and that, short of stopping them moving around the countryside, it would be hopeless even to try to prevent the transmission of orders, or of warnings. Tench would not change his mind. He asked me whether there were some centres where meetings took place. The answer was yes.

'Destroy them,' ordered Tench, and that was that.

'This would result in the death of some innocent people,' I argued.

'Destroy them,' was the answer. Tench did not want to know about the possibility of political and other repercussions. Destroy was his order.

I then tried the ultimate argument.

'If I do this, you will put me in the position of the SS or Gestapo, who destroy human life on orders. Would you like to be responsible for the same type of orders as those of Himmler and Co.?' I asked.

'I shall forget your question and its implications. Destroy. That is an order.'

'Not b. . . . likely,' I said to myself when I left the Inspector. Tench was, in fact, quite remote from what was actually happening in the District. He could not know all the details and, provided the action I was envisaging made quite a stir, Tench would be satisfied that his orders had been carried out.

There was, in one of the villages, a house known to shelter, and to be the meeting place of, communist and bandit groups. The household was headed by a woman by the name of K., whose sons were convicted criminals and who was directing the activities of several thieves and robbers. I ordered the surveillance of this house and then its destruction, together with its occupants, at a time when it would be full. The decision was not an easy one to make. I had no court of law, yet I had as far as possible to keep order and to protect people. K.'s house, its occupants and their activities, had been an eyesore for quite a time. Now, I felt, was the time to kill two birds with one stone: to satisfy the orders of the High Command and to get rid of this eyesore.

Two weeks later the job was completed. Four people were killed and the house burnt down. One of our men was also killed. The house was a fortress and all the occupants very well armed. The action made quite a stir in the District and I was able to report to the Inspector that his orders had been duly carried out. Tench seemed to be quite happy about the outcome of his order to 'disrupt the bandits' communications', but I was not, and waited anxiously for repercussions.

By now work in the District was progressing satisfactorily, although two events took place which provided me with some headaches.

The first had to do with S., my second-in-command. For some weeks I had received reports about alleged abuses by S. of his position as the Director of Aid for Refugees. Proof was impossible to obtain, but my Staff were not happy about the situation and strained relations between S. and members of the Staff began to hinder the smooth working of the Command.

The situation had to be resolved one way or the other, so I summoned S. and quite frankly explained to him my dilemma and asked him what solution he could suggest. S. was amazingly decent about the whole thing. He denied all the allegations and said that these were unavoidable in his position. Taking into consideration the good of the Organization, so laboriously set up, he offered his resignation as second-in-command. I accepted it, but asked S. to continue to cooperate with me whenever need arose. He willingly agreed. At the next meeting with my Staff, I announced the resignation of S. and, with the full approval of everyone present, appointed

77

Blackie as my second-in-command. After a while the work was again running smoothly, with such a common under-standing of all ideas and purposes that I was able to delegate much of my authority to the members of my Staff with complete confidence.

The second problem arose through the action of my Adjutant. On the advice of S., and to reduce my wanderings about the District, I had appointed as my Adjutant a young reserve officer. He did his job quite well. When I had to send him to Warsaw with maps showing the possible sites for air drops, I asked the young man to go and visit my grandmother. I suspected that the old lady was herself engaged in under-ground work, just as she, of course, suspected me, but on the only occasion we saw each other after I left Warsaw we did not speak of it, nor did we ask each other any questions.

The old lady thought, however, that a messenger from her grandson must be a hundred per cent trustworthy fellow and she started talking to him freely, without mentioning any names, about me or my family. Actually I learnt no details about this talk but could draw inferences after the young man returned from Warsaw. People began to question my right to be in the position I was in, saying that I had very little Polish blood in my veins, and that I had no right to lead Poles in their fight against the Germans—a silly and irritating argument. This attitude was very effectively countered by Blackie, who put forward the following proposition: if I was a foreigner, Poles should appreciate the fact that a foreigner was willing to risk his life every minute of the day for the common cause. That effectively stopped all gossip about me and my origins. Nevertheless, I had to dismiss the young man from his duties. He went over to the Nationalist Party and, because of his big mouth, became another source of danger to me.

A radio transmitter, sent from Warsaw, had been installed at Cmielow, with Karol (Charles), a radio operator from the former River Prypet flotilla, working full time transmitting coded messages to London via Sweden. A squad of well-armed men was always with him, although the probability of the transmitter being discovered by the German detector vans was remote. When they used to appear, they were rapidly spotted and Cmielow was warned to stop transmission.

Coded radio messages arrived from Warsaw nearly every day via a special messenger network established separately for this purpose.

In May, 1943, the first air drop had been received near Ozarow—two officers, two million dollars and some arms and ammunition. The briefing of the two officers was appalling. Before being sent to Warsaw they had to be coached on how to behave. Yardley perfumes and English cigarettes had to be confiscated, clothing checked for labels, etc.

The son of the solicitor Polikier, who was staying with the Halperts, had to be moved from his billet. He looked very Jewish, the whole neighbourhood knew him as a Jew and he was sitting on one of the main arms depots near Ozarow. His move proved to be the near undoing of me, as later developments showed.

Ponury had been recalled to Warsaw. His place was taken by his second-in-command, Lieutenant Nurt. He and his men were still in the foothills of the Holy Cross Mountains, licking their wounds and awaiting arms from Warsaw. However, two loads of arms and ammunition had been intercepted by the Germans with the loss of four lives among the escort. There was a leak somewhere. My intelligence network went to work and it was soon established that one of the officers of the group, while on leave at Kielce, had been visiting Gestapo Headquarters. On his return to the group he was arrested. During his trial he confessed and was summarily executed. That was the only instance I knew of in which a Polish officer turned traitor.

Then, some time in July, one of the platoon commanders in Ozarow was kidnapped by the so-called People's Army (by now under Russian command) and shot dead. The long-expected move by the Russians and the communists had

79

started at last. Tarzan received orders to track, and to finish off, the group who had perpetrated the execution. Tarzan ambushed them successfully a week later and in the resulting fight all twelve were shot dead. Two of Tarzan's men were wounded. A few weeks later another officer, Count Szembek, was murdered. This time I asked Nurt to move into action. Nurt tracked down the killers and successfully engaged them. The result: twenty-one dead. That was a language the communists understood. They stopped further executions and combined all their remaining forces into one group about two hundred strong, taking very strong precautions against any surprise attack. At the same time radio broadcasts from Moscow were shedding crocodile tears about the 'fratricide' going on in Opatow.

The communists now changed tack and tried to contact me with a view to our joining forces under the aegis of the People's Army to fight the common enemy. Nothing was mentioned about the fact that, until then, and thereafter as well, the People's Army had not taken part in a single action against the Germans, not only in the province of Kielce but right across the country. Yet Moscow Radio and the underground communist news sheet revelled in descriptions of clashes, always victorious, with German forces in the German-occupied parts of Poland. In fact, these communist groups and the Germans were both engaged in trying to destroy forces led by true Poles. And so I sat tight.

By now I had been promoted to Lieutenant-Commander, not necessarily because I had earned my promotion, but because the High Command in Warsaw decided in their wisdom that all District Commanders should have at least the rank of army Captain. That was an amazing decision. The Polish Armed Forces, pre-war, were an amazing assortment of officers from the three occupying powers, Austria, Germany and Russia. All had different characteristics: those from the German forces were strict disciplinarians, rigid in their opinions and outlook; those from the former Austrian Empire

80

were somewhat effeminate and very strict about being addressed at all times with their full titles. Not only the officers but all civil servants had the same attitude, which extended also to their wives. I well remembered the occasion when, before the war, I had been presented at a social occasion to Mrs Maria Kasprzycka, the wife of the then Minister of War, General Kasprzycki. When I addressed the lady as *Pani* (Madam), she said, 'Lieutenant, I have to remind you that I am the wife of a General and should therefore be addressed as "Madame la Générale".' (She and her husband were from Galicia, the part of Poland under Austrian occupation). I apologized and started to insert the words 'Madame la Générale' into nearly every sentence. Fortunately the lady was very nice and had a sense of humour. After half an hour of our conversation she started laughing and asked me to address her simply as *Pani* Maria.

The senior naval and army officers from the Russian forces were all rough characters, with a touch of the dare-devil in them, full of cavalier spirit and often speaking a sort of pidgin Polish. After the 1920 war with the Soviets, the powers that be decided to do something about their poor command of Polish and courses in Polish were established. I always liked the story about a class attended by greying colonels and majors. During the break the instructor, a young university graduate, had written on the blackboard in large letters '*Pan Tadeusz*'. That was the title of the epic poem of the great Polish poet Mickiewicz, a standard text in schools. When the class returned from the break, the instructor asked them, 'Who wrote this?' There was dead silence. Eventually the instructor asked one officer in the front bench, 'Perhaps you could tell us, Sir?' The officer answered seriously, 'I can give you my word of honour that nobody from our group wrote it.' The unofficial version of this story goes further. Apparently one of the officers went over to the instructor and whispered into his ear, 'Listen, young man, I suspect that Major so-and-so did it. Last week he broke a window and did not own up then either.'

81

The result of these various backgrounds was that many officers had a chip on their shoulders; even junior ranks believed in privilege without special responsibility. All had two common qualities, however. They loved their country and had unlimited courage. Nevertheless the rank of Captain in the Army was not necessarily a reference as a good commander of the Underground, a position which entailed so many responsibilities in so many areas. This is why I knew that the decision was a daft one. When I received the notification of my promotion, I refused to accept it, reminding the High Command that I was a naval officer and had, therefore, no qualifications for the rank. I was, however, somewhat apprehensive about the possible trains of thought of the people in Warsaw. Eventually, after a few weeks, I was notified that I had been promoted to the rank of Lieutenant-Commander in the Polish Navy.

How silly this order of minimum rank was, was demonstrated a few weeks later. The District of Konskie, about fifty miles west of Ostrowiec, had been organized and put into shape by a reserve sub-lieutenant, a local man and a village teacher.

He was appointed C.O. of the District as early as 1940. Now, instead of promoting him to the rank of Captain, which he richly deserved, Warsaw sent to the District an Army Captain to replace him and to take over his command. The man did not know a thing about conditions in the country and in particular about the conditions which existed in the District of Konskie. That was the District which had suffered most from the stupid Hubala episode early in 1940, when two thousand villagers had been killed. The Germans at that time had already had the opportunity to become well acquainted with the terrain and had their security forces strategically placed. Within three weeks of the arrival of the new C.O., he and his staff were arrested and the old C.O. had to take over what was left.

In a brilliant action by the Konskie partisan group of Szary

(Grey), the prison was stormed and all the prisoners set free. The action was, however, followed by further mass arrests and deportations to the concentration camps. I did not know whether the Army Captain had been left in his new command or not. I only knew that it was very bad for the Commander to be remote from the rank and file of his members.

One of our safe houses was on the Goloszyce estate belonging to a certain Mr Julian Leszczynski, who was married to an English lady of Polish descent. The estate was situated near the road from Opatow to Kielce, running along the southern foothills of the Holy Cross Mountains. Mr Leszczynski was small, wiry and strong, with piercing brown eyes. I felt secure and happy at his house. He had his own security force: every night a guard was posted on the first-floor balcony of the manor house. The guard was unarmed, but just behind him, within easy reach, there was an arms cache under the floor: two rifles, a few hand-grenades and a machine pistol, bought for quite a large sum of money from a German soldier. Yes, the Germans, too, were trafficking quite heavily in arms.

Mrs Leszczynski introduced an English flavour into the life of the household—no seeming concern about the arms hidden in the house, English marmalade and toast for breakfast. I had no idea where she was able to get hold of oranges. The marmalade always seemed to be freshly made!

In January, 1943, I had a meeting at Goloszyce with the Regional C.O. After the meeting a messenger came from Moczal, the *Kreishauptmann* at Opatow, that a big shoot was to be held next day in the forest of the Goloszyce estate and that Mr Leszczynski was to provide a few guns to make up the necessary number. The German Army had no warm uniforms on the Russian front and the shoot was to be held to provide as many fox and hare skins for the front as possible. Mr L. was to provide the two guns for which he had a permit and the rest would be brought in by Moczal's party.

Mr L. said to me, 'Why don't you come? I doubt if they will be asking me about your genealogy. I shall arrange to join them as late as possible. Would you come? You and them—it would be fun.'

I felt reckless and agreed. We decided that it would be useless to carry any arms except the guns we had, and so the next morning Mr L., two of his men and I started for the rendezvous on the edge of the forest. The road and all the area around the forest was full of German soldiers, SD personnel and Gendarmerie. Moczal must have mobilized half the German army to guard his party against the Russian partisans, who were supposedly operating in the District.

We were not searched. Mr L. scrounged a few dozen cartridges for our 12-bore guns and off we went to take our position for the first beat. The beaters were people from the neighbouring village of Backowice.

Each of us was flanked by a German soldier. I could not at first understand what the soldier was there for. The reason soon became very clear: I managed to shoot stone dead the first hare which happened to saunter towards me in the deep snow. Without waiting, the soldier ran into the line of fire to pick up the hare, without listening to my warning that he should not endanger his and my life in this way, but should wait until the end of this particular shoot. He did the same with the second hare. I had had enough. During the second shoot I started missing with every shot. Some of my shots went so wide that at one time I was afraid that the soldier would notice my efforts to miss. Fortunately he did not, and after two hours he left me and went to stand by the side of somebody else.

I was enjoying myself, but at the same time there was a feeling of unreality. Except for the German soldiers flanking us, it seemed as if I were transported back in time to winter days before the war, when I used to go hunting with my father and his friends in the Prypet Marshes in the east of the country, where the frost in winter was severe and the snow was deep. We used to go to the region where General Carton de Wiart, a Britisher, used to come hunting, saying that there were only two places on earth where one could really enjoy the shoot:

one was India and the other the Prypet Marshes. He had a sort of hunting lodge in the most remote part of the marshes. The lodge was accessible only on foot or by boat. In it he had installed a bath and generator! Epic tales went around the countryside about the transport and the installation of these amenities. I had always visualized the General sitting in the evening by a blazing log fire under some sporting etchings hung on the wooden walls, with a drink in his hand, reading *The Times*. All this seemed a very long time ago. Now, towards the end of the day, I was practically on my own, on one of the flank positions. I suddenly saw a beautiful fox, running laboriously through the snow. I thought about the General and about what he would have had to say about my shooting the fox. So unsporting, my dear boy! But Irena needed a fur to keep her warm and Roman knew of a furrier, so I shot it. It dropped into a deep mound of snow. My guardian angel came running over to ask what I had shot. I said that I had shot at another hare and that I had missed again. He went off, disgusted. When he was gone I winked at one of Mr L.'s men and told him to collect the fox after the shoot was over. He did, and so ended my shoot with the Germans—and that was how Irena acquired, in due course, a fox fur in 1943!

Later on, in January, Irena and I took lodgings a block away from the Gestapo headquarters. Nearby was a room in which there was an automatic mangle, an appliance always used in Poland to make laundry smooth and easy to iron. As usual, the mangle was being used by many neighbouring housewives; it was a focus for an inexhaustible amount of gossip and so Irena had an additional source of all sorts of information about what was going on.

In February, 1943, SS General Kutchera, the Warsaw Gestapo chief, was shot in broad daylight in Warsaw. The news came from the Gestapo secretary that on Hitler's orders hostages would be taken in every town in the General Gouvernement and publicly hanged. The quota for Ostrowiec was thirty-five men.

I ordered all my Staff to leave Ostrowiec and to spread this news as quickly and as widely as possible. Everyone should know about the danger. Irena and I also left Ostrowiec and went to Jeleniec, the Halperts' residence, which was well inside the forest, north of Ostrowiec.

The next day a battalion of SS with armoured cars and personnel carriers entered Ostrowiec and during the night thirty-five people were taken at random from their homes and thrown into the town prison.

I had to arrange a meeting with my Staff to discuss the situation. Fifteen of the arrested were known to belong officially to the Home Army, though none of them had any special function. For the whole day my Staff and I discussed our dilemma: whether or not to spring the arrested out of the prison? The SS battalion was billeted about three kilometres from the prison. The prison itself was near the town limits and within easy reach of the friendly forest. It was guarded by twelve SS men and ten Polish policemen. By that time, even without Ponury's or Tarzan's help, we could muster enough of a force to break into the prison and free all the prisoners. But then what? Another battalion of SS would come and one hundred instead of thirty-five hostages would be taken and executed. News was reaching Poland of the heroic stand of Tito's partisans in Yugoslavia and of the appalling losses among the civilian population resulting from partisan actions. Of course Tito was a pupil of Stalin and for him human losses did not matter as long as he could achieve what he wanted. I and my Staff felt differently. All losses had to be balanced against any gain. We knew that by springing the existing hostages we would have to inflict heavy casualties on the Germans. The terror would then simply escalate. At the same time we could not afford to take on all the forces the Germans could bring into action. Our decision was therefore to let these thirty-five men die. It was not an easy decision and we parted with heavy hearts.

Two days later, thirty-five gibbets were erected in the

market square. At about noon the square began to fill with a silent crowd. I felt it my duty to witness the execution, and I too was in the crowd.

At noon the thirty-five prisoners were brought to the place of execution. They were not blindfolded. The gibbets were surrounded by SS, and Jews were brought from Sandomierz to carry out the hanging. I knew that the proceedings would be detestable.

With their hands and feet tied together, the condemned were simply hoisted one by one by the noose around their necks until they were a few feet above the ground and there they were left to choke slowly to death. The sight was not a pleasant one, with the victims jerking and twisting and revolving, round and round and round.

The sky was clear except for a white cloud above the square, hanging over the crowd and over the gibbets with the dying men, and over the jeering and laughing SS men. I was filled with a feeling of awe, because in this cloud I could feel the presence of my, and of their, God, of God witnessing the evil in Man and the suffering of his children. I knew then that God could be found in other places than in consecrated churches.

When the bodies were finally still the market place slowly emptied in dead silence. Only the SS men were left to finish what they had to do, to see that there were no survivors.

Feeling in the town was so intense that the Gestapo Chief, Soldau, deemed it necessary to issue an unofficial statement that he personally had had nothing to do with the hangings, that the decision was not his and was entirely out of his jurisdiction. He was rightly afraid of possible reprisals against him.

A few days later Tarzan's group ambushed and killed a German General (if I remember correctly it was General von Speer) and four of his staff officers on the road near Ozarow. Tarzan was crafty enough to leave a Russian soldier's cap and a few rounds of Russian ammunition at the scene of the ambush.

Where he got them I had no idea and did not ask. The Gestapo were told, indirectly, that the attack was perpetrated by Russian paratroopers and no reprisals followed. Fighting two enemies at a time could, after all, have some advantages.

VIII

The Jewish Problem

THERE WERE ABOUT ten thousand Jews in the District. Before
the war they were concentrated mainly in Ostrowiec and
Opatow. The Germans had moved them all to Ostrowiec, so
that when I arrived the town had a section set aside for Jewish
occupation. They lived in crowded conditions, but were able
to move around the town, the distinctive yellow Star of David
on their breast. They were, of course, all Polish citizens and,
after I had sorted out my organizational problems, I began to
think about the problem they presented.

First of all I tried to recall all I knew about them from history
and from my past experiences, mainly before and during the
Russian Revolution of 1917.

The history of the Jewish people is in itself a very complicated one, and history also determined, at least to some extent,
the position of Jews in Poland before the war. All of this
constituted a most complex problem.

The first Jews to settle in Poland probably came from the
area between the Rivers Volga and Don, which had
established Judaism as a state religion in the eighth century
A.D. While the Jews were expelled from England in 1209,
from France in 1306 and 1394, from Spain in 1492, and several
times in the fifteenth and sixteenth centuries from Germany
and other European countries, in Poland they were always
accepted. Prince Boleslas the Pious in 1264 and King Casimir
the Great in 1334, 1354 and in 1362 granted them privileges.

They could therefore develop their own culture and customs. These were typical of their race, but alien to those of the Slavs in general, and of the Poles in particular.

True, in the eighteenth century there had been an attempt at assimilation. In 1755 Jacob Leibovitch Frank founded the Messianic sect of Frankists. In 1760 Frank and his followers were christened, and in the seventies Frankists numbered about 24,000, existing not only in Warsaw (where they numbered about 6,000) but in other parts of Poland, in Romania, Czechoslovakia and Southern Germany. All were eventually assimilated completely in their respective milieus. Many prominent Polish families, including the Halperts, were direct descendants of Frankists.

Because of the partitions of Poland in the eighteenth century, all attempts to guarantee equal rights for the Jews failed. The policy of the Russians was to play the Poles against the Jews and vice versa. The Kosciuszko uprising in the 1790s saw the participation of the Jews in the national struggle for independence: the symbol of this participation was Berek Joselewicz, a legionnaire, eventually a colonel of the Principality of Warsaw, who was killed in a skirmish with the Austrians at Kock on 5 May, 1809.

As far as I knew there were about 3.5 million Jews in Poland at the start of the war, constituting about ten per cent of the population. The intellectual and bourgeois Jews—doctors, teachers, scientists, industrialists, bankers and big business-men—were accepted by all, and differed little from the rest of us. My family had good friends among them: Dr Ryskin, from Orscha; General Dr Wulich, the only Jew to rise to the rank of general in the Imperial Russian Army; Dr Mucha, a brilliant surgeon who in 1915 saved my life by a daring operation; Professor Dr Bruner of the Warsaw University, a great friend of my grandmother. My parents' tradesmen in Warsaw, the butcher, the grocer, the baker, etc, were all Jews. Some aspects of trade were virtually monopolized by the Jews—the meat business, for example. All meat for Jewish consumption had to be kosher, and all animals were killed ritually under rabbinical supervision. Thus all the abattoirs in Poland were run by Jews. Since the Jews were not allowed to eat the hindquarters of cattle, only the hindquarters came on the open market, and an idea was current that forequarters were of inferior quality. As a result no cheaper meat cuts were available for Gentile consumption. By 1938, there was a growing awareness of this problem, which was giving rise to antisemitic feeling. A little, but it was there.

The lower classes of the Jewish population, the small traders, tailors, cobblers, etc, were all Orthodox Jews. From what I could remember of my childhood and from what I could observe in the autumn of 1939, the Orthodox Jews, the fundamentalist believers, were all anti-communist. The intellectuals, on the other hand, were often in favour of communism. Often humiliated by the antisemitic faction of the populace, alienated from their own society and yet not always fully accepted by the Poles, they were perhaps subconsciously seeking in communism the 'Kingdom of Heaven'. Many leaders of the Bolshevik Party in Russia were Jews: Trotsky, Kamenev, Zinoviev, to name but a few. From my childhood I remembered the Bolshevik commissars—they were all Jews. It was frightening to see how they revelled in their power of life and death. I saw the same phenomenon in 1939, when I was caught by the Russian invasion of the eastern part of the country: nearly every commissar I had the misfortune to meet was a Jew.

I remembered something else as well. In 1939 a young soldier, a Jew, was dying in my arms, his leg nearly shorn off and suppurating with gaseous gangrene.

'Lieutenant,' he said, 'I was so afraid when we were ordered to attack the Germans. But when I thought about what they were doing to my country and to us Jews, I went forward and killed and killed and killed. I was wounded and I know that now I am dying. Will you please hold my hand and pray for me to our common God?'

A few minutes later he was dead.

I had to talk with S., Blackie and Drake about the Jews. We met at S.'s house and I asked them to tell me in turn what they thought about the Jewish situation and what we could do to help them, if anything. Each of them talked at some length. The gist of what S. and Blackie had to say was that the attitude of the Jews towards the Germans had probably been conditioned by centuries of persecution. They knew all about what was going on in Germany. They knew about the extermination camps. They deplored their present situation in Poland. However, they seemed to believe that this, too, would pass and, provided they did not antagonize the Germans, they would survive. It seemed as if they were used to the idea of being a martyr nation. What they wanted was to be left alone.

Drake was more specific. Officially he worked in his father's office. His father was a Notary Public and, after Poland surrendered, he came into frequent contact with nearly all the leaders of the Jewish community, who were trying to sell their properties. They knew that sooner or later their possessions would be expropriated. Drake had talked to most of them, sounding them out as to whether any of them would go into hiding and join some kind of resistance movement. None of them had shown any inclination to do so, nor had they seen fit to provide any names from among their community of those who would be willing to do so. Leave us alone, they used to say; we do not want to take any risks. But what about the concentration camps? What about Dachau, Auschwitz and other places of extermination? These places, was the answer, are for you as well. We Jews do not want to take any risks. We know that, if we show any sign of resistance, the end will come very quickly. Drake had to abandon his probings. After all, he did not know whether they might not decide to ingratiate themselves with the Germans by telling them about his propositions.

92

The same attitude, I thought, as Spiegel's when going to his certain death: clinging to a straw which existed only in their wishful thinking.

And so nothing could be done for them or with them for the time being, except to monitor the few Jewish families already in hiding within Polish households.

In January, 1943, Ostrowiec was suddenly saturated with SS and with special detachments of the Gestapo and Gendarmerie. I was spending the night in Ostrowiec when I was awakened before dawn by shots, shouting and general commotion in the streets. All the Jews in the town were being rounded up. Several were killed resisting arrest. Next morning the pavements in the Jewish quarter of the town were spattered with blood. All Jews, women and children included, were rounded up and in the morning they were marched towards Sandomierz, where a proper ghetto was being established. The sight of the struggling column, hurrying along the road, was horrific. Old men who could not keep pace were being shot with glee by the SS men. So were old women, and children torn from the arms of their mothers. Eventually they all disappeared behind a curtain of fog.

A few Jews managed to escape. Some days later Drake reported that a group of four Jews had been spotted in the forest around the villages near Ostrowiec. They had two revolvers and were demanding food with menaces. Another group of five had been detected near Opatow. When I saw Drake I told him that his men should contact the two groups and, provided that they submitted to the authority of the Home Army, they should be taken care of. If they refused, they should be ordered to leave the District, which already had to carry the burden of several partisan groups.

From the Ostrowiec group only one Jew agreed to join the Underground. The other three refused, without being able to offer convincing reasons. They left the District and disappeared. Where they went, we did not know.

Then I received the disturbing news that the Jewish group wandering around Opatow had been slaughtered in a clearing in the forest in the foothills of the Holy Cross Mountains. We did not know the culprit and I was not anxious to find out.

IX

The Political Parties
and the Consolidation of the
War Effort by the Nation

BEFORE MARSHAL PILSUDSKI'S coup d'etat in 1926, the political
scene in Poland was strewn with various factions of the main
political parties, the Polish Socialist Party (P.P.S.), the Polish
National Party, comprising a centre and an extreme right
wing, and the Polish People's Party, the party of the peasant
population. After the coup these parties lost their power and
the dominant party which emerged was the B.B.W.R. (the
Non-Party Block of Cooperation with the Government). It
was popularly called the Colonels' Party. During the war all
the old parties became active again and all, except the
B.B.W.R. were somewhat apprehensive about the Polish
Government-in-Exile in London. Nevertheless a National
Government Executive was formed in Warsaw and the Home
Army C.O., General Grot (Rowecki, who took over from the
founder of the official resistance movement, Z.W.Z.,*
General Tokarzewski), acting on the instructions from the
Underground Executive, tried for a year to consolidate the
Home Army's position by absorbing into it all the armed
wings of the political parties. The slogan of the Home Army

* The Organization for Armed Warfare.

High Command was: Let us first have a home; then let us furnish it.

I had no problems with the Socialists, who from the beginning had willingly cooperated under my command. The centre of the National Party had no armed forces, while the extreme right had formed the National Armed Forces and refused to cooperate at all. More of them later.

My main problem arose with the Peasant Battalions of the Peasant Party. Although no recognizable Peasant Battalions existed in the District, it was predominantly a peasant one and the Party objected strongly to having their men put under the command of an officer of the Home Army, which still carried the stigma of the Colonels' Government. Nevertheless, urgent orders were sent to me to try at all costs to take the Peasant Battalions under my wing and to induce the Peasant Party to enter into full political cooperation.

One day I was informed that the local Chairman of the Peasant Party wanted to see me. We met. He was a young lawyer and started by saying that in no way could his Party cooperate while I was in command. All my Staff were aristocrats and landowners and in consequence he could not agree to follow the orders of his Central Committee and place himself and his men under my command. I asked him to wait for two days until all my Staff could assemble and he could meet them.

We spent those two days discussing the problems that would face Poland after the war. His predictions concerning the development of rural life in Poland were rather pessimistic. His main concern was that whenever sons of a peasant family went to a college or university, they very seldom returned to the land, and as a result no technological, social or cultural advances could be achieved, no new methods, no new ideas introduced into agriculture. On the whole, he and I got on well together.

When I was able to present my Staff I asked them to tell us about their social backgrounds. It transpired that all were first-

or second-generation educated descendants of peasant stock. He could not overlook this fact and I could feel that he was taken aback by these revelations, which he had not expected. He then started on another tack. Since the majority of the population of the District were peasants, he could not see any reason why he, as their leader, should accept a position as my deputy, as agreed by his Central Committee in Warsaw. From this position I could not shift him.

I then hit on a bright idea: 'Would you be agreeable to take over the command of the District?' I asked.

The answer was an eager yes. This would mean the end of the command for me, but I could see no other way out. I had to wait upon events.

I explained the situation to my Staff. All agreed that it seemed the only way out of the impasse. And so I went back to the young chairman and, after a long introduction, in a general sort of way and without mentioning any organizational details or names, I suggested that we go straight out into the field and begin to work together, before command was officially handed over.

There were, at the time, a number of problems to be solved and decisions to be made. Another air drop had been notified; its date had to be fixed and transmitted to London, its security arranged, and the drop itself would need to be supervised. A decision had to be taken on whether or not to spring some prisoners, two of whom belonged to an independent group, from the Opatow jail—what force to use, when and how. To augment our funds, a raid on the sugar depot in Ostrowiec had been suggested: decisions needed to be made on whether or not to carry it out; and if so, how it would be done, when, and under whose leadership. A lorry-load of arms had been brought into one of the villages and was hidden in the church spire. How should we distribute these arms, and to whom?

The correspondence with Provincial Command had to be taken care of. Orders had to be analysed. Reports had to be discussed, written and sent to Provincial Command. Intelligence reports, coming from Drake, in Ostrowiec, and his deputy, who operated in the countryside, had to be processed and sent to the Provincial G.2.

In three days, using bicycles, horses and carts, the District Peasant Party leader and I covered at least one hundred kilometres, sleeping, sometimes in beds, sometimes in barns, sometimes hungry, sometimes eating our fill, talking all the time, discussing, making decisions, giving orders. In the end the young chap had had enough and somewhat sheepishly said that after careful consideration he would be quite happy to put his forces under the command of the Home Army. I objected to his decision very strongly, but he was quite adamant; we parted and that was the last I saw of him.

I did not, of course, tell him that the amount of travel and the number of meetings we had during those three days were quite unnecessary. By that time there was such an understanding between all the members of my Staff and myself, such a unity of ideas and of purpose, that most of the problems we had had to deal with could have been resolved by those directly concerned with them. I could delegate my authority to such an extent that it had been suggested that I was not doing my job properly, and was operating solely through my Staff as intermediary. These voices had been very effectively stilled when my men pointed out that if an organization can be run without the manager breathing heavily over the shoulders of his staff, it must be efficient.

The first raid on the sugar depot was a success. The storekeeper provided all the necessary information and two tons of sugar were taken away at night, with the storekeeper left trussed like a chicken on the floor, with a bump on his head. No reprisals followed. Two weeks later, however, when another raid on the stores was taking place, the new storekeeper, although he had agreed to help, lost courage and informed the Germans. The party was caught by a platoon of Gendarmerie and one man was killed, though the rest managed to escape. Sadly, the man killed was Stas.

Fortunately he had been living with his mother, a widow, and was not officially registered at this address. The Germans had some idea of his identiy, but they were not sure. So they took his mother to the mortuary. She was a beautiful woman in her mid-forties. Her husband had been active before the war in the Socialist Party and had been killed in action in the first week of the fighting. She knew very well that if she recognized the body of her son she herself would be arrested, tortured and interrogated about all her son's acquaintances. She knew that she could not risk recognition. She had already been warned that her son was dead and that she would probably have to go and identify him.

She calmly went with the Germans to the mortuary. Without a trace of emotion she looked at the body of her only child and said, 'I never saw this man in my life.' The Germans let her go and abandoned all further investigation.

Rumour was again rife in the town that Russian para-troopers had been operating in the District and in Ostrowiec itself. The Germans now directed all their efforts to finding and destroying the Russians. But they had no luck and lost heart.

When people in a small town are closely knit by circum-stances, as was the case in Ostrowiec, it is very easy to spread rumours or information. The speed with which news travels through the grapevine is fantastic. One example was the time when I had bicycled through Ostrowiec after the arrest of Maria, a trip supposedly known only to my Staff.

Sashka was still chasing me and I was trying very hard to finish him off. However, we missed each other continually, though we both had good intelligence networks. The thing was that, although Sashka controlled a band of about two hundred men, he was making no effort to attack the Germans or to sabotage their war effort. This was in line with the news from beyond the Vistula, where large groups of the commu-nist-led People's Army were operating under the command of Russian officers who were either escaped PoWs or had been parachuted into Poland. These groups were concentrating on fighting the partisan groups of the Home Army and left the Germans well alone. The Germans apparently did the same, so the losses of the Home Army east of the Vistula were heavy. I could count myself lucky that Sashka had insufficient support to do much harm.

In August, 1943, Drake was arrested. His brother, who was in the executive of the High Command in Warsaw, had taken part in the abortive coup on the main Warsaw prison, Pawiak. Although wounded, he escaped and made his way to his parents in Ostrowiec. He was tracked down and was arrested with his brother. I decided to spring him from prison. I had the means now, and Drake was too important a member of the organization to lose and, besides, he knew too much.

But the day before the coup was to take place Drake's parents sent me a note imploring me to do nothing. They claimed that the Germans had no proof against either man, that they, the parents, had enough pull with the Germans (Soldau was often a visitor at their house) to free them eventually, and that springing them from jail would definitely aggravate the danger for all concerned. I made contact with the two young men, who were asked their opinion and their wishes. Both Drake and his brother said that they would prefer to risk deportation. They had not been tortured and the worst that Soldau promised was the concentration camp. They both preferred to risk this than problematic liberty, with its associated problems for their family. I postponed the break-out. In discussion with my Staff I found the pressure to be so relentless that I eventually decided to abandon the action altogether. Three days later both brothers were deported. Soldau must have been well bribed because they were not sent to the concentration camp but to forced labour in Germany.

With Drake no longer with us, I was forced to appoint a deputy, as Head of Intelligence, a man known as Smith. One of Smith's tasks was to take over the archives established by Drake, which had not been found by the Germans, and to start a comprehensive record, of all the actions of the communists and their bands in the District. The records were to include details of all killings and robberies. People could argue that these bands needed to 'confiscate' provisions in order to survive, but when two of these bands were liquidated, carts were found filled with women's underwear and jars of fruit preserves, hardly consistent with a fight for survival. The records were kept up to date, and are still hidden in the District.

X

Interlude: Irena

IRENA, MY WIFE, companion, friend, lover, tower of strength
and source of peace; resourceful and clever, with an uncanny
ability to sum up people's characters, an ability derived not
from her mind but from her heart; a woman who took life in
her stride and always made the best of it. She was patient and
kind, never jealous or boastful, arrogant or rude. She did not
insist on her own way, was not irritable or resentful. She bore
all things, believed in right, hoped for all things and endured
all things. By the grace of God she was always there.

She was of medium height, with beautiful auburn hair, eyes
which looked blue when she was in good spirits, dull grey
when under stress. She was not a beauty but had a certain *'je ne
sais quoi'* which made men turn their heads. She had broad
shoulders and strong arms, from rowing and playing tennis,
muscular legs from mountaineering and skiing. And she could
have easily competed with Helen of Troy in wine cup
modelling.

A graduate of Warsaw's Technical University, she worked
before the war in one of the War Office research institutes. We
were married in August, 1937. In 1938 she bore me a son,
Andrew. In 1939 we found ourselves in the Russian-occupied
zone of Poland. She engineered my release from the Russian
prison. When I was arrested by the Germans in November of
the same year, she was left on her own.

Andrew was living with her sister in a suburb of Warsaw,

with his great-grandmother and his nanny. This arrangement allowed Irena enough freedom of movement to earn some money for living expenses.

Through her contacts with her University colleagues she managed to buy on the black market a container of palm oil, the raw material essential to the soap-making process. Her 'soap factory' was set up thirty kilometres from Warsaw. At least twice a week she had to take the soap to town. It was in two suitcases, weighing about twenty kilos each. She had, of course, to travel by train. That year the winter set in quite early and there were days when she had to travel, carrying the suitcases, in temperatures as low as −25°C.

The task was not an easy one. One evening a Wehrmacht soldier, seeing her staggering under the weight of the suitcases, offered her his help. She was scared stiff, but the soldier, without waiting for an answer, took the two suitcases and carried them to the station, about a mile and a half away, without ever asking her why they were so heavy. She thanked him. He saluted smartly and then vanished into the night.

Unfortunately, the soap-making venture did not last long. In January, 1940, on her way into Warsaw with the soap, she slipped on some rubble in the street and severely damaged her knee, which had been injured before the war. She was bedridden for about six weeks, lying flat on her back in an unheated room on the first floor of a house partly demolished by bombs. Even so, she did not give up and very quickly established herself as a black-market broker in hard currency, gold, jewellery and commodities. Every morning her bedroom looked like a general store: loads of flour (bought from the Germans at black-market prices), 5-dollar pieces, gold and diamond rings, etc, were on sale and she had to find buyers, which she always managed to do.

In February, 1940, she got a message, saying that I had escaped from the military hospital. To her great surprise she also received from me a large leg of pork, which came in very

103

useful. I had managed to buy it by selling the gold from my signet ring, and the pork was intended as a farewell gift. I was on my way out of the country.

By this time her black-market activities had become too well known and for safety reasons she moved back to her sister's house and to Andrew. Another source of income had to be found, so she started working on the assembly line of a factory in Warsaw making torch batteries, which was owned and run by one of her colleagues from the University. She started work at 7 am , which meant getting up at 4.30. She had to walk one and a half miles to the station in all weathers and then travel on a train which had no windows. Sometimes she drank vodka to keep her warm. This situation lasted until June of that year.

A week before my appointment to the command in Opatow, the Kielce C.O. sent me to Warsaw to discuss a few problems with someone from the High Command. I had been given only one address for making contact. When I objected, I was told that it was all right, that the address was that of a dental surgeon in one of the main streets and that it was one hundred per cent safe. Reluctantly I went to Warsaw and there, in front of the house where I was supposed to go, was a Gestapo car! I did not know quite what to do, but then I remembered the private address of one member of the Staff at Kielce who had been transferred to Warsaw. Rather unwisely, I went to his address, which was in one of the huge students' hostels attached to the Warsaw School of Economics. His flat was on the first floor. I went up and knocked on the door. The door opposite opened and a frightened face made desperate signs to me to go away. I turned round and had started to retrace my steps when, rounding the corner, I saw two men walking towards me, both in Gestapo black-leather coats. I passed them nonchalantly and left: I was lucky: they had been waiting at my friend's flat and just before I arrived they had presumably gone for a walk round the corridors. It was a lesson to me: never approach any address without reconnoitering it beforehand. I decided not to try to see Irena that day.

In June, 1941, however, having established myself more or less solidly at Opatow, I contacted Irena and asked her to go and live with my cousin near Sandomierz. My cousin, a Ukrainian, had a small farm near a village on the Vistula. The Ukrainians have been implacable enemies of Russia throughout all history and the Germans considered them as allies in the fight against Bolshevism. In their advance through the Ukraine in 1941 they were met as liberators, with the traditional bread and salt. It was Hitler's stupidity which made the Ukrainians turn against them. Nevertheless, the Germans managed to form one Ukrainian Division, consisting mainly of those Ukrainians living within the Polish borders before the war, and the rest were favoured in various ways. My cousin, being very anti-Soviet, was courted all the time by the Germans. The Gestapo used to pay him frequent visits, trying to induce him to work with them. He always refused, saying that he was not a political animal and was first and foremost a Polish citizen. Nevertheless the Germans remained very friendly towards him and his house seemed a perfect refuge for Irena and our son.

He lived with his wife, the daughter of a professor at Warsaw University, his son, his mother-in-law and another cousin in a dilapidated manor house eking out a meagre living by cultivating vegetables and keeping a few cattle, sheep, goats and pigs, which could find just enough grazing in the ravines which crossed his land.

And so Irena, having lost the baby conceived during her only stay with me at Kielce, went to live with my cousin. She endured, without complaint, six months of living with my cousin's mother-in-law. When we were offered shelter by Dahlia, she was happy for a while. But although our son Andrew was well cared for, Irena was hardly tolerated. Whenever guests arrived, and a good meal was being prepared, she had to retire to her room for a meal of groats or soup. Always Irena had the feeling of being a 'poor cousin'. Actually, that was what she was, of course, but the feeling was not a very nice one.

When she and I were asked to leave, we were both fortunate and very grateful to Dahlia that our son could stay behind. For Irena, this was the start of a continuous wandering, an anxious odyssey from one place to another. What belongings Irena had, she left with Dahlia. These included the signet ring with my family crest and a sealed envelope containing my surname. It did not take long for Dahlia and her friends to decipher our surname from my family crest.

Irena had with her a small suitcase containing two spare shirts for me, her spare blouse and some underwear. She also had our fur blanket. I had told her always to be ready to move at fifteen minutes notice. She never complained; she was always ready to go anywhere as my messenger. She never knew if she would see me again. By God's grace I always managed to come back to her from my wanderings, finding solace and peace in her arms. At night, hugging each other in narrow beds, or in the hay, or in the straw, we always used to pray, thanking God for the day just passed, asking Him for a safe tomorrow and good health for our relatives and for all those whose existence was continually in jeopardy.

She was never afraid, or at least she never showed it. She used to wander into the forest and the fields to try to supplement our diet with berries and edible fungi. She was usually hungry, sometimes even thirsty.

In 1943 we were offered an abandoned forest hut on the Halperts' estate. Irena had plenty of fungi to pick and she made some berberis juice. One day she had an offer from the neighbouring forester who wanted to use the lean-to of the house to slaughter a cow and proposed to divide the proceeds. She agreed. The cow was slaughtered, the meat sold and for the first time since the start of the war she had some money to spare and some meat left. She decided to give a party for the Halperts. They came gladly and Mr Halpert remembered the

1. Irena Sagajllo just before the War.

2. Witold Sagajllo before the War.

3. Kennkarte – Identity Cards issued by the German occupying forces during the War.

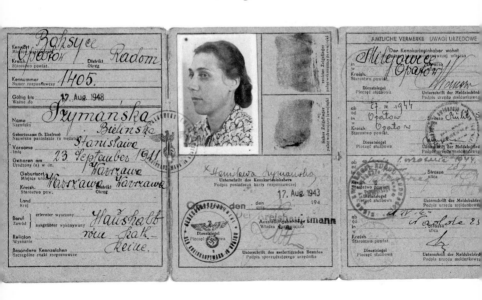

PAŃSTWOWE
LICEUM ROLNICZE
MĘSKIE i ŻEŃSKIE
W DZIKOWIE

DYREKTOR

Dzików, dnia *29.5* 194*5* r.
p-ta, st. kol. Tarnobrzeg

Zaświadczenie

L. dz. *124* /194*5* r.

Niniejszym poświadczam, że ob. Szymański Witold ur. 30.3. 1905 zatrudniony jest jako wykładowca w tut. Liceum Rolniczym od 1 kwietnia 1945.

Dyrektor:
mgr. J. Krzyżanowski
(mgr. J. Krzyżanowski)

4. Certificate of employment at the State Agricultural College near Tarnobrzog, dated 29th of May 1945.

5. Irena Sagajllo in 1943.

6. Wiltold Sagajllo in 1940.

Vyslanectví Československé republiky ve Varšavě.
Légation de la République Tchécoslovaque à Varsovie

Varšava, dne 19 září 1945

P r o p u s t k a .

Vyslanectví Československé Republiky ve Varšavě žádá
zdvořile, aby československé pohraniční úřady umožnily vstup
krátkodobý pobyt a výjezd zpět do Polska p.
Stanislawa S Z Y M A N S K A
narozená   23.IX.1911
která jede do   Prahy a Plzně
za účelem   rodinným
Platí do 30.X/října/ 194

Za Vyslance:

Československý spolek v Krakov
č. 1680/II/45-H

ČESKÝ TĚŠÍN
HLAVNÍ MOST
2 0. IX. 1945
PŘÍCHOD

Předseda:

Vyslanectví Československé republiky ve Varšavě.
Légation de la République Tchécoslovaque à Varsovie

Varšava, dne 19 září 1945

P r o p u s t k a .

Vyslanectví Československé Republiky ve Varšavě žádá
zdvořile, aby československé pohraniční úřady umožnily vstup
krátkodobý pobyt a výjezd zpět do Polska p.
Witold S Z Y M A N S K I
narozený   30.III.1905
který jede do   Prahy a Plzně
za účelem   rodinným
Platí do 30.X/října/ 19

Za Vyslance:

Československý spolek v Krakově
č. 1674/II/45-H

ČESKÝ TĚŠÍN
HLAVNÍ MOST
2 0. IX. 1945
PŘÍCHOD

Předseda:

7. The fifty dollar Czechoslovakian visa issued by F. Wesely of the
Committee for Czechoslovakian refugees in Cracow. Three days later
Wesely was arrested.

Národní Výbor v Plzni – National Council at Plzeň

Народный Комитет в Пильзени

Národní Výbor v Plzni nemá námitek, aby pan /paní/

Народный Комитет в Пильзени не имеет возражений, чтобы тов.

The National Council at Plzeň has no objections that Mr./Mrs./

граж. Станислав Сциманска,

............Stanislav S z y m a n s k a,............

odcestoval do   České Kubice.

уехал в   г. Чешские Кубице.

leave for .....Česká Kubice..............................

za účelem   návštěvy.

с целью   посещение знакомих.

to ....visit...............................

Plzeň, 26.9.   19 45.

Пильзень, 26. 9. 1945. г.

(razítko: OKRESNÍ NÁRODNÍ VÝBOR V PLZNI)

Národní Výbor v Plzni – National Council at Plzeň

Народный Комитет в Пильзени

Národní Výbor v Plzni nemá námitek, aby pan /paní/

Народный Комитет в Пильзени не имеет возражений, чтобы тов.

The National Council at Plzeň has no objections that Mr./Mrs./

............граж. Witold S z y m a n s k i,............

граж. В итолд Сцыманскн

odcestoval do   České kubice.

уехал в   г. Чешские Кубице.

leave for ......Česká Kubice..........................

za účelem   návštěvy.

с целью   посещение знакимих.

to ....to visit...........................

Plzeň, 26.9.   19 45.

Пильзень, 26. 9. 1945. г.

(razítko: OKRESNÍ NÁRODNÍ VÝBOR V PLZNI)

8. The Permit to go by rail to České Kubice (at the border with the American Zone) 'to visit acquaintances'. Issued by the National Regional committee at Pilsen on 26th September 1945.

čislo
Number ....30305.........
Номер

dne
date Sept. 24th 1945.

ДНЯ

Jméno Mr. Witold SZYMANSKI
Name ... Mrs. Stanislava "-"
Фамилия and Andrzej child

platné do
valid till Sept.27th 1945.

действительно ПО

Red Army and US Guards at the demarcation line are requested to

Прошу советских и американских офицеров, разрешить

permit the above named free passage trought the demarcation line

переход через демаркационную линию вышеуказанному лицу.

v
at.......Rokycany..........
ИЗ

do a z
to and from ....P l z e ň..........
B

Platí (jednou vícekráte)
good for ....once................
действительно

čislo legitimace
No.of identification card ....
номер удостоверения   1674/II/45-A
                        1680/II/45-A

1st. Lt . SCHONBORN
Liaison Officer
Czechoslovak General Staff

Офицер связи
Чехословацкой Республики

Povolenka pro cizince pro pře=
chod US=SSSR demarkační čáry.
Neplatno pro SSSR a US vojíny.

Не действительно для со-
ветских и американских
солдат.

This Pass is not valid for
US of Red Army military personal.

9. The fifty dollar pass to cross the Russian–American demarcation
line.

```
POLISH  CONTACT  TEMA  7
H.Q.  XX  CORPS  U.S.ARMY
                    APO  340


                                                5 November 1945


    To whom it may concern.

            It is certify, that P.W.x Capt.W. S A G A J L L O
    is authorized to wear the American uniform of Khaki colour.
```

```
                                            Capt.S.A.PONIATOWSKI
                                            Polish P.W.Contact Officer Nr.45
                                            H.Q.XX Corps U.S.Army  APO 340
```

10. The permit to wear a khaki American uniform after a near arrest.

```
                                        COMD 2 POLISH CORPS
                                            No 977/Evac/46
                                        --------------------
                                            5 FEB 46


                    C E R T I F I C A T E
                    ============================
    This is to certify, that

            1.Mr. SAGAJŁŁO Witold
    is authorized to enter ITALY in order to join his
    relatives in the 2 POLCORPS.
```

```
                                    COMD 2 POLISH CORPS

                                    W. A N D E R S
                                    Lt.Gen.
```

11. Certificate of authorization for Witold Sagajllo to enter Italy.

013851 ✳ **D. P.**
Andrzej **Identification Card**
M

Name SAGAJLLO   Date of birth 5.VII.36 Age 9
Name   Geburtsdatum   Alter
Height 119 Weight 22 Hair l.blond Eyes blue
Größe   Gewicht   Haar   Augen
Nationality Polish   D P Registration No. G02871123
Nationalität   D P Registratur No.

Andrzej Sagajłło
D P Signature / D P Unterschrift

Scars or identifying marks
Narben oder besondere Merkmale
Mothers—spot on
left underarm.
                    Fingerprint R. Thumb
                    Fingerabdruck R. Daumen

Issued at Murnau   Camp No. 2539/3 Date 22.V.46.
Ausgestellt in   No. des Lagers   Datum

Repatriated to   Date
Rücktransportiert nach   Datum

H.TOP
Director UNRRA Team 194
Name and Rank of Issuing U. S.
Camp Commander or UNRRA Official
Name und Dienstgrad des Lager-
Kommandanten oder der UNRRA Behörde

Validation date   Official Stamp
Gültigkeitsdatum   Amtlicher Stempel

12. Andrew's Identity Card issued by UNRRA in Murnau, Bavaria, May 1946.

INSTRUCTIONS.

1. Repatriation and validation entries must be authenti-
   cated with official stamp.
2. This card valid only at D. P. camp or place where issued.
3. This card must be carried on the person at all times.
4. THIS CARD MUST BE PRODUCED IN ORDER TO
   DRAW MONTHLY RATION CARD.

ANORDNUNG.

1. Rücktransport- und Gültigkeitsvermerke müssen mit
   amtlichen Stempeln beglaubigt werden.
2. Diese Karte ist nur in dem D. P. Lager gültig, in dem
   sie ausgestellt wurde.
3. Diese Karte muß man immer mit sich führen.
4. DIESE KARTE MUSS ZUR MONATLICHEN LEBENS-
   MITTEL KARTENAUSGABE VORGEZEIGT WERDEN.

AGPS-3317-2-46-500 M 33539

feast for a long time. The menu consisted of a *consommé* with French dumplings, boiled beef with horse-radish sauce and potatoes. For dessert millet with cream and berberis juice. Mr Halpert was really happy.

The next day, having spent the night at Jeleniec, she found on her return to the house that the place had been ransacked. We did not know by whom, but Mr Halpert kindly invited us to establish ourselves at Jeleniec.

This stay with the Halperts was probably the happiest and the most relaxed period of our lives during the war. Irena was treated as one of the family. She was never hungry. She was never cold. She could have a bath whenever she wanted.

There was excitement one day at Jeleniec. They were expecting a visit from Princess Sapieha and, although the Halperts were rather well connected, a princess, and of the royal blood at that, was a Princess, and they were snobbish enough to want to meet the Princess in style.

I came to Jeleniec after supper, which consisted, I was told, of *consommé*, pork and buckwheat served, like chestnuts, with cream. Besides the Princess, a few other guests were present, all ladies, and, except Irena, all in evening gowns. The late arrivals were myself, Prince D.-L. and a certain Mr Horodyski.

Prince D.-L. belonged to a good family from eastern Poland. His wife had been born a German countess, from Upper Silesia. In 1921 her father had opted for Poland and for the rest of his life he paid for this with innumerable petty restrictions from the German government—his estates remained within the Third Reich. He died before Hitler came to power, but his son, Princess D.-L.'s brother, was one of Himmler's aides-de-camp. Twice he came to visit his sister on the Prince's estate, bordering on to Jeleniec, but lying in the district of Starachowice, to the west.

Prince D.-L. toed the patriotic line officially. His palace housed several families, refugees from Poznan. These refugees even used to have their meals at the same huge dining table as

107

their hosts. However, while the Prince and his family were eating as well as before the war (plenty of meat, venison, wines, butter, poultry, etc), the refugees at the same table had groats, borsch, potatoes and black bread. In the nursery quarters there hung a huge portrait of Hitler, and the children had to say their prayers in German. They could live well because, not only was the Prince selling wood freely on the black market, but also all the official allocation to the forestry workers of cigarettes, clothing and alcohol, the Princess used to *sell* to the workers for whatever they could pay in kind: poultry, eggs, milk, etc. For these activities the Prince received twenty-five lashes. But this is another story.

Mr Horodyski, having lost all his property in eastern Poland, was living on a small estate belonging to his wife, on the eastern bank of the Vistula. He had been a well-known horseman before the war and his two sons were active members of the Home Army in Warsaw. He himself took an active part in the movement in his Tarnobrzeg district. Above all, he was a gentleman.

This particular evening, when I arrived at Jeleniec, I followed the Prince and Mr Horodyski into the great hall. I was then able to observed something which gladdened my heart.

Sitting in a row were Mrs Halpert, Princess Sapieha, Princess D.-L., Mrs Szymanski, my wife and the rest of the ladies. All were in evening gowns except for Irena, who had on the second best of her blouses (the other one was drying) and her mended skirt. Both garments, although clean and well pressed, showed a considerable amount of wear and tear.

The first to be introduced to the company was the Prince. On being introduced to Princess Sapieha, he bowed deeply and kissed her hand; then he kissed the hand of his wife; then in a condescending manner he produced two fingers to touch the hand of Mrs Szymanski; then he bowed and kissed the hand of Mrs Dygat (she was the daughter of another aristocrat, Count Zamoyski) and eventually he proceeded nonchalantly to shake the hands of the remaining ladies.

108

Mr Horodyski being behind the Prince, I had the opportunity to watch him. On being introduced, he bowed and kissed the hand of Princess Sapieha, produced two fingers for a desultory shaking of the hand of Princess D.-L., then bowed and kissed the hand of Irena, then of Mrs Dygat and so on. I followed suit, observing with some glee the controlled fury of Princess D.-L.

Jeleniec stood at the edge of a hundred-acre field, planted at that time with buckwheat. The house was surrounded on the other three sides by forest, smelling of pine, humming with bees in summer and deep in snow in winter. The house itself was in two parts: the old one, built of larch, containing Mr and Mrs Halpert's apartment, the dining room and all the household offices; and the new one, built of red brick, a two-storey edifice attached by a short passage to the old part of the house. The ground foor was a huge hall, with Mr Halpert's African big-game trophies, and a huge inglenook fireplace in the middle heated by a large factory-type cast-iron stove. A gallery with a library ran around the first floor. The second floor contained several bedrooms and two bathrooms.

Jeleniec was full. Besides the owners, there was a Roman Catholic priest, a refugee from Poznan; Professor Wiechowicz of the Poznan Conservatoire; Eugenia Uminska, the celebrated Polish woman violinist; the son, Zygmunt Halpert; Mrs. D., wife of the very well-known Polish pianist living in Paris, and her two daughters Barbara and Sophie; and lastly Mr and Mrs Polikier, mentioned earlier.

During the day everyone was left to his or her own devices, but in the evening, after supper, everyone congregated in the great hall. There was music, bridge, chess or just talk. On a few occasions I stayed at Jeleniec, I had the opportunity to play bridge or chess with Mr Polikier. He was a brilliant chess player and used to beat me without much effort. Professor Wiechowicz would try to guide me to an understanding of modern music. He had not much success. When Irena stayed

109

there, she took lessons in Russian from Mrs Polikier, which proved to be very useful to her in the future.

It would be difficult even to list all the safe houses Irena and I stayed at. In the winter of 1944 she decided to take Andrew back from Dahlia. Although he had been taken good care of, he had begun to lose weight and to suffer from his separation from his mother. I found them a safe house on the outskirts of Opatow; they moved there in February, 1944, and stayed until August, when they had to move. But this is another part of the story.

These last lodgings of Irena and Andrew in the District were probably the poorest of all the accommodation Irena had: just one room in an attic of a house owned by one of Roman's men. The room was about ten feet by ten; and could hold only one bed—in which Irena would sleep sardine-wise with Andrew —a small table, one chair and a small kitchen range.

Andrew was unwell, not only because he had been separated for a long time from his mother, but also because he had worms. With the help of our District Medical Officer Irena soon got rid of these worms and then Andrew started to improve dramatically. The small house stood about twenty yards back from the Opatow-Kielce road and Irena lived undisturbed except for one night during which she was awakened by unusual noises and activity in the yard. When she looked out of the window she witnessed the unloading of a quantity of arms which were taken from two farm carts and carried into the barn. She also saw that the road towards town was sealed off by armed men, hiding in the ditches on both sides of the road.

A month or so after they had moved into Opatow, I had an opportunity to go and see them. When I entered the room I reeled back from the heat. I was glad I had come. Andrew was standing on an upturned box by the kitchen range. The top of the range was white hot and the boy was trying to fry an egg in a frying pan nearly as hot as the top of the range, managing to hold it with some sort of thick rag. Irena was in bed, semi-

110

conscious and shivering with rising fever. This was her second day in bed and she had a severe bout of flu.

After helping Andrew with his frying and seeing Irena start to eat, I left to see Roman and tell him of Irena's plight. He told me to leave everything to him. And, indeed, after I had been back for an hour or so, the landlady appeared, very apologetic. She claimed that she did not know anything about Irena's flu and assured me that from then on she would take care of Irena and Andrew. I left them, with peace of mind.

XI

The Beginning of
the End

1943 PASSED RELATIVELY quietly in the District. More and more
arms were bought. Roman's relationship with Herr Donat,
the SD commander, proved, one night, to be very useful. He
was taking a full cartload of arms and ammunition acquired
near Starachowice to Opatow, about twenty miles west of
Ostrowiec, hidden under a pile of firewood. It was late and he
was in a hurry. Near Ostrowiec he was stopped by a foot
patrol of four gendarmes. Fortunately for Roman he was
always cool-headed and he did not panic. The gendarmes
recognized him as a friend of Herr Donat and asked if they
could have a lift back to Opatow. It would save them waiting
for transport and at the same time would provide Roman with
an escort after the curfew. Roman gladly invited them to
climb up next to him on to the pile of wood. He produced a
bottle of vodka, some bread and sausage and off they went on
their way to Opatow. Roman reached home late that night,
having deposited his escort at their barracks.

In an isolated house near Opatow the Gestapo discovered
the printing press used for the National Party's underground
news sheet. Donat and a few members of his Staff raided the
house. They found one man busily engaged in printing the
news sheet. After a scuffle he was arrested and Donat was left
to take him to the jail. Donat shot the man dead, supposedly
while he was trying to escape. That was the official version.

Next day Donat came to see Roman. He was very apologetic and said that he had to shoot the man to prevent any repercussions or further arrests. He was quite right to do so and his apology was accepted.

In August Donat mounted an abortive attack on one of Sashka's group, the only German operation against the communists that I knew of. The usual pattern of German field operations throughout the country was to concentrate on the Home Army partisan groups. Sometimes the Germans and the Russian-led communists were quite close to each other, each in turn attacking the Home Army partisans while leaving the other alone. It seemed that German pride was hurt by the existence of partisan groups among an already conquered nation.

Unfortunately Donat was killed in the skirmish, the only casualty. His successor, appointed straight away, was quite a different man—ruthless and very pro-Nazi. Two weeks after he took over the SD at Opatow, he was shot dead by Andy.

Sabotage operations were now restricted to burning the harvested corn ready for thrashing and delivery. One day I was on my way back from Sandomierz after a meeting with Tench and my counterpart in Sandomierz, Captain Black (Czarny). On my own territory I was always notified of any SD or Gendarmerie patrols going into the countryside. Now I was in Sandomierz territory, driven by Walter, Andy's chief executioner.

Coming round a bend in a large copse of birch trees, we were surprised by a mobile Gendarmerie patrol. We were stopped, twenty machine pistols pointing at us from the truck. This is it, I thought. Two gendarmes came over to us to demand our document. One of them started to frisk me. I had some documents from the meeting, together with my pistol, hidden in my right boot. When his hands were approaching my boots I asked him in German if he wanted me to take my boots off so that he could inspect them. The gendarme stopped frisking me and said *Nein*, went over to the officer who was checking the documents, took the papers and gave them back to me. I asked him what it was all about. He answered that bandits were burning the harvest and that they had to investigate. We parted and I arrived safely at Opatow, where I was staying at the time. My false papers had proved to be satisfactorily convincing.

The battle for Stalingrad was won and lost. Then came the battle of Kursk. The Germans were in retreat all over the Eastern Front. The Home Army High Command began to finalize Project STORM in which the Home Army would come into the open to attack the retreating German Army on every front.

I was notified that I would have to prepare for a particularly important meeting with a special envoy from Warsaw. The meeting was to be attended by Tench, Black and myself. Strict security measures were to be enforced; lodgings and meals would be provided.

I arranged the meeting at the priest's house in a village near Ozarow, about five kilometres north of the main west–east road leading from the west to the bridge over the Vistula. All roads leading to the village were discreetly sealed off by about two hundred men belonging to Witold.

In the evening the envoy was picked up at the station in Cmielow. The priest, who used the pseudonym Rogala, was host at quite a lavish supper, during which it transpired that the envoy, a lieutenant colonel, had been head of the Artillery Department at the Ministry of Defence before the war. He was very anxious to know all about the security arrangements. I told him not to worry and that, in case of emergency, the Germans could be contained long enough for the colonel to make his escape by any of the several routes available.

At about midnight we all retired for the night. The village seemed to be dead. I went out. Immediately Witold appeared and together we went to inspect the security arrangements. They were adequate to hold of a platoon of well-armed Germans. But if as many as a company of them made a

114

determined effort to capture us all, the chances of the colonel escaping by any of the routes available would have been rather slim. However, every one of us was used to living on the brink of disaster and none of us, except the colonel, seemed to be very concerned about what might happen.

The meeting started the next day after breakfast. After outlining the general idea of STORM, the Colonel began to assign to Black and me our tasks in the operation.

Mine was to destory the bridge over the Vistula and to hold the left bank of the river at the ford upstream of the bridge. This ford had to be defended at all costs. I felt that this was in the realms of fantasy.

'Sir,' I started to object, 'the whole operation is based on the assumption that the German Army will be retreating in complete disarray and will be as anxious to surrender as it was in 1919. The success of my men will depend entirely on the Germans' morale. Don't you understand, sir, that I can bring into action only about four hundred men, with twelve machine-guns, one anti-tank gun and two 80mm mortars with only a few rounds of ammunition. True, the left bank of the river is quite steep but the ford can be successfully defended only if the Germans attacking it are completely demoralized. If not, if they really want to force the ford, there can be little chance of holding them. They will probably have tanks and artillery, and in any case they'll have enough fire-power to make short work of liquidating our resistance. As to holding on, regardless of losses, I have heard about such orders being issued by Hitler. Our losses in this war have already been appalling and what could we gain by holding the Germans at this ford when all the might of Soviet Russia is only a few steps behind them? By sacrificing a few hundred men we may satisfy the political aims of our allies, but we will not change Russia's policy towards us. A determined attack by even a battalion of the German Army will wipe out my four hundred men in a few hours at most and their sacrifice will be utterly wasted.'

115

'Never mind the losses, the outcome of the fight or the politics,' answered the colonel. 'These are your orders, and you will obey them.'

'Yes, sir,' I answered. 'But under protest.'

Now Black's objectives in the Sandomierz District were discussed. Although numerically strong, Black's men had only about forty-five rifles, no machine-guns, no workshops for making hand grenades and a very limited quantity of ammunition. On the other hand, the town of Sandomierz was the training centre for German sappers. Their barracks on the outskirts of the town held a total complement of about three thousand men. It was fortified with typical German ingenuity with barbed-wire fences and machine-gun emplacements giving cross-fire covering all the approaches. The terrain consisted of flat cornfields and provided no shelter whatsoever.

I had had an opportunity to reconnoitre the barracks quite thoroughly when I had to take refuge in Sandomierz when things were too hot for me in my own District. I stayed in Sandomierz for a week, with Sophie Z., one of my cousins. She, her husband (a diabetic) and their two boys were refugees from Upper Silesia, which had been incorporated into the Reich. They were sheltering two Silesians who had fled from their homes to the General Gouvernement in order to avoid being drafted into the German Army. One of them was a butcher. They made a living by illegally slaughtering pigs, curing bacon and making sausages for the black market. It was a dangerous business and I could stay with them for only a few days. From their house and garden I could study the whole of the barracks and watch what went on at the Gestapo Headquarters just two blocks away. After the meeting with Tench and Black, which nearly led to my capture on the road to Opatow, I had intended to stay with Sophie for the night. Approaching the house I could see from the distance that it was deserted, and a few passers-by were looking at me warningly. I turned back. Later, Black told me that Z. had been arrested. Sophie said that as I was walking towards their

116

home, she was delivering a food parcel to her husband and her heart stopped beating when she saw where I was going. The house was under observation by the Gestapo at the time. Her husband died a few months later at Oswiecim (Auschwitz).

To return to the meeting with the Colonel. He asked about the situation in Sandomierz and the prospect of a successful action. The strength of the Germans, the fortifications, the barbed wire, the lack of cover and most of all the fact that Black had at his disposal only a few rifles were all explained to him. The Colonel listened carefully and then said, 'Nevertheless the orders for the District of Sandomierz are that the Sapper Training Centre is to be attacked and captured, regardless of losses.'

'You must be joking, Colonel,' I said, and started to laugh.

'Commander,' answered the Colonel, 'your remarks, your behaviour and your tone of voice show a lack of discipline which I cannot tolerate. The Sandomierz C.O. will carry out the orders as they have been explicitly given.'

I looked to Tench for help. It was not forthcoming.

'Do you mean, sir, that in spite of all that has been explained to you, the men will have to attack?'

'Yes,' said the Colonel.

'Two hundred men with forty-five rifles across an open field, against a fortified complex manned by three thousand men, all professionals, with machine-guns, mortars and artillery?'

'Yes,' answered the Colonel. 'And if there are not many rifles, there are always flails and scythes. Remember that.'

A deadly silence followed this pronouncement. Tench and Black were speechless. And then for the first time in my life, I completely lost my temper. All the pressures I had had to endure and all the frustrations I had experienced combined to overwhelm my self-control.

'You are either a fool, Colonel,' I said, 'or a traitor. You have survived the war until now, so you cannot be a fool. But by issuing such an order you seem determined to play into the

117

hands of both the Germans and the Russians. They have been trying their best to liquidate as many of the polish Resistance as they possibly could.

'With respect, Inspector,' I said to Tench, 'I hereby terminate the meeting and will ask the Colonel to leave.'

The Colonel was fuming.

'How dare you?' he shouted. 'The meeting will continue and you are under arrest!'

'Just try. I am withdrawing all the guards and security forces and I am leaving the meeting. If you want to stay you do so at your own risk as from now.'

I left the room. Tench came out after me. 'Are you crazy, Felix? Don't you know that you have jeopardized your career?'

'What career? Do I have one? Do you, for that matter, under the communists and the Russians? The best we can both expect is to have a few square yards of earth in the cemetery. If we are not to be thrown on to a rubbish heap, that is. You talk about a career. You have known me for four years now, and I would have thought that by now you should know that I have never thought of a "career", as you call it. Don't you realize that I have been doing a job, fighting for an ideal, for a cause? And once you start to expect a reward for fighting for an ideal, you forget about the ideal. You are just a mercenary. I hoped that you would understand this, and that you would feel the same.'

'Yes, but after all, we are in the Services and the Colonel came from the High Command in Warsaw and we cannot throw him out of the meeting like that.'

'Then why did you keep your mouth shut at the meeting? You didn't say a word, either for him or against him. If you are on his side, you can have my resignation straight away.'

'I do not agree with the Colonel,' said Tench. 'But what could I have done? Nothing. I do not accept, and never will accept, your resignation. They will chuck you out in due course, but it will take time.'

118

'Be that as it may. But for the moment, will you please go back and tell the blighter that the security forces have been withdrawn and that you cannot guarantee his safety any more.'

Meekly, Tench went back and I had the satisfaction of seeing the Colonel leaving in a hurry for the station to catch the first train to Warsaw.

I stayed the night with the priest. In his long, black cassock, with bushy eyebrows and aquiline nose, he reminded me of a picture of the Grand Inquisitor I had seen somewhere. He was very intelligent and did not, somehow, fit the role of priest to a small village. I knew that he was a member of Drake's intelligence network, but his knowledge of human nature and of world-wide events and history exceeded, by far, those of a simple cleric. I felt that he must have been, or perhaps still was, a member of the intelligence network of the Roman Catholic Church and that for some reason he was in hiding. We talked well into the night about all kinds of subjects. In the morning Rogala said that he would be celebrating Mass and he invited me to join in the service. I said that I would be quite happy to do so, but I warned him that although I would be glad to take communion, I had to tell him that I was a Protestant. His reaction was surprising. For all his education, knowledge and intelligence, he showed by his reaction the extent to which the Roman Catholic clergy were conditioned in their outlook and beliefs. He was flabbergasted. His eyes bulging in astonishment, he burst out, 'But you talked as if you were one of us!'

For a long time we looked at each other in silence. After his outburst Rogala seemed ill at ease. I was outwardly quite calm, but inwardly was seething with suppressed anger. Although the priest was much older than I, I could not resist having my say.

'Father, we are all at war. Whatever their faith and beliefs, people are being killed, imprisoned and tortured. And yet you, a servant of God, with all your education, dare to differentiate between people by using the word "we" and by

119

implication thinking in terms of "they" or "you". "We" and "they"—this is the battle cry of communists: we, the workers, the proletariat, you, the bourgeoisie, the capitalists. Before the war we had innumerable official or unofficial political parties: the government party, the socialists, the democrats, the people's party, the nationalists and so on and so forth. They all differentiated between "we" and "they". History has shown us what differentiations like this between gentry, burghers, peasants, could do and did do to our country. Throughout all our history, instead of emphasizing what was common to all of us, we have emphasized the differences. I assume that by "we" you meant the Roman Catholics. But you and I were born first as Poles and after that we acquired our religious beliefs. Could you not look at me as a Pole first and then as a Protestant? Could you not consider all we have in common first and only then taken into account all our differences? We were not talking this evening about religion. We were talking as two Poles, and the fact that you remarked that I was talking the same language as "we", shows clearly that what matters is what we have in common.'

Rogala was quite contrite and said that he had not really meant to use the word 'we'. After all, he had been living in this small village for a few years now. All the people around him were Roman Catholics; all of them considered that what was Roman Catholic was good. To them, every Protestant, if not a German, was at best a foreigner. Protestantism was for them a heresy; all Protestants were heretics to be shied away from. No wonder that he, a priest in this village made this *lapsus linguae*, for which he very sincerely apologized.

After all this we went to the church to attend Mass. He did not ask me to take communion. It would probably have been too much for him.

The affair with the Warsaw Colonel made me disheartened and even more apprehensive of the future. I could foresee much blood being spilled in senseless ventures for the sake of unsatisfied ambitions and thwarted power.

120

Winter came and then the spring of 1944. The training of all the local forces was intensified. Charles, the radio operator, was worked to exhaustion, sending endless coded messages to London. I asked Warsaw for a Military Cross for Charles. I received no answer, although I knew that in Warsaw radio operators were being decorated for valour after having sent ten thousand coded groups.

Eventually consent came from Warsaw to form a separate partisan group of fifty men in the District. I appointed Lieutenant Mruk to lead them and went to see them off; they were very well armed, with five heavy machine-guns and five machine-pistols, and they had plenty of ammunition and money. We had a church service before setting off and I rode with them for a few miles that night before they disappeared into the Holy Cross forests. Communications between Mruk and Nurt had already been established. The communists had to behave now; they had already become more civilized—they did not kill or even loot any more. After all, they had lost twenty-one of their men after the last incident and now, with both Mruk and Nurt operating in force, they would have lost many more if they had continued in their normal fashion.

During the winter of 1944 I had another problem to face. The National Armed Forces, the fighting wing of the extreme right wing of the National Party, became very active. Their political philosophy reflected the dilemma the Polish nation was in.

It was a fact that the Polish nation was caught between two evils: Hitler's extermination policy and Stalin's similar tactics. The Germans could be assumed to be degenerate Europeans, the Russians were totally alien. What should the Poles do? It was not only a moral problem, but was also a problem of the survival of everything Western civilization had evolved over a thousand years. The political philosophy of the National Forces was as follows: the defeat of Nazi Germany could be taken for granted, the main threat to the Polish nation was presented by the Russians, who had to be fought, and

121

weakened, to such a degree that they would not be able to oppose the Allies, irrespective of Yalta, Teheran, etc. The weakening of Stalinist Russia must be achieved by all available means. The end result of this philosophy was that while the Allies were hand-in-glove with one evil, Stalin, the National Forces were collaborating with the other, the Germans. They were partly armed by them and accepted their help. However, while French or Norwegian collaborators were actively engaged in suppressing all forms of native resistance, the National Forces never cooperated with the Germans against the Home Army.

This did not mean that they took much action, if any, against the communists. All the same I was happy to see another force working against the communists. Many a time, when resting at night in one of my so-called 'safe houses', I was awakened by shots and shouts of 'Sandacz, Sandacz', my pseudonym in the District. They knew about me but they did not even try to betray me. Not being officially pro-German, they were tolerated by the population and, after Mruk and Witold had disarmed two of their groups, all dead drunk, they too began to behave in an orderly manner. But they made it more difficult for me to move around. I had to change my quarters every few days.

How remote from the grass roots of the nation was the High Command in Warsaw was again demonstrated by the following example. One day I had word from Dahlia that a certain Mr K. wanted to see me. In great secrecy she told me that Mr K. was a special emissary from the High Command in Warsaw, sent to investigate and to report on the situation in the country and the feelings and morale of the population.

I knew Mr K. very well. He had an estate south of Opatow, one of the larger ones in the District. He was a member of an aristocratic family, a Papal Chamberlain and very arrogant in his behaviour. From what I knew of him, he had never been to his stewards' homes and I doubted if he had ever spoken to any of the workers on his estate. How it was possible for this man

122

truly to appraise the feelings and the morale of the population was completely beyond my comprehension. The only morale and the only feelings he could understand were those of his own class. And yet he was a delegate of the High Command who would, in all probability, base their policy on, or at least allow it to be influenced by, his reports. Why it was necessary was beyond me. Tench and I submitted monthly reports about the situation, the morale and everything else which concerned the District. These reports went to the Provincial Command and I knew, from my work there, that they were incorporated into Provincial reports and then submitted to Warsaw.

I had my meeting with Mr K. It was a social, rather than an official occasion: drinks, calf's liver wonderfully fried with plenty of onions, and real coffee. We chatted about everything and nothing and Mr K. went back to his estate and then on to Warsaw. Where and how he made his appraisal of the situation in the District I never discovered.

One evening in November I had a meeting in a house at the foot of the Holy Cross Mountains. After the meeting I was invited to stay for the night, an invitation which I gladly accepted. Besides myself there were four people at the evening meal: my host, his mother, about eighty years old, and two aunts, who both looked even older than the mother. It was Saturday and after supper I was asked if I would be kind enough to play poker with the ladies for very low stakes.

'They have so little fun at their age and with all this terrible war and the weather . . .' said my host.

Since the stakes seemed to be very low indeed, I, warm-hearted fellow that I was (I also liked the game and was not too bad at it) agreed, and we sat down to play around a green-baize-covered table. It was quite a scene. The wind was howling outside; a huge stove radiated heat; a paraffin lamp, hung low over the table, emphasized the shadows, its mellow light illuminating the three old ladies, like three old witches, warily watching every turn of the cards. All were smoking

123

and the packet of cigarettes I had brought with me was soon finished. The ladies then started to smoke their own brand—dried horse-chestnut leaves. The room was soon like a bandits' den, the heavy smoke making me cough and sneeze. All this did not seem to affect the old ladies. They played all night and by Sunday afternoon I was finished. I had lost all my money, I was reeling with fatigue, had a parched throat and bleary eyes. But the old ladies were still going strong and were very reluctant to end the session.

In May the blow fell. I was relieved of my command of the District. The official reason given was that the decision had been made reluctantly (consoling words), but had to be made because of my opposition to the communists, who were allies, and because of the broadcast on Moscow Radio about the fratricide going on in Opatow. Because the Russians 'are still our allies', I had to give up my over-all command and was left with my independent partisan group, which was being placed at the disposition of Tench.

I was delighted by this decision. After all, I had been underground since February, 1940, when I had escaped from the hospital and had had more than enough of hiding, striking, retreating and hiding again. Now, I thought, I would be fighting in the open, although against whom I was not quite sure. I knew my men. They were well armed. I knew the terrain and now, I thought, I would be able to put to the test my abilities in the field. The 'glory' was just around the corner!

There was a nagging doubt, however, in my mind. My command of the partisans could be, and was, related to the fact that I had been the instigator of 'fratricide'. How would this affect me? I put the thought aside and was happy.

In due course I met my successor, an insignificant-looking infantry captain. I felt apprehensive about him. He came to the District from neighbouring Starachowice. He had lasted there only three weeks before being 'burnt'. Before that he had been the C.O. of the Konskie District, further west, where he had lasted for six weeks. On that occasion all his Staff were arrested and he himself only narrowly escaped. I wondered how long the chap would last in his new post. Also I could not stop thinking about how it was that this sort of record did not convey to the men at the top that something was amiss.

The reason was probably that the Home Army, having lost so many men since the war started, was short of manpower. After Stalingrad the Home Army was swamped with applications from officers in hiding who suddenly wanted to join the Underground. Orders from Warsaw were quite explicit about them: they should not be admitted to the ranks of the Home Army. I had the opportunity to deal with such an applicant, a Commander in the Polish Navy. When I interviewed him, I found an elegantly-dressed gentleman, exuding health and self-confidence. When asked what he had done all these years, he answered that he had escaped from the Germans, had been able to obtain false papers and for the last three years he had been running a saw mill, confiscated by the Germans from a Jew, on the Germans' behalf. Now, he thought, the time had come to offer his services to 'the cause'.

'The cause started in 1939 and you have had plenty of scope to serve it in the last four years. Now it is too late for you. Go back and continue to serve the Germans by running their sawmill. Good-bye.' I did not shake hands and the Commander left.

But orders were orders and after I had introduced the new C.O. to my Staff and had gone with him to each of the District commanders, and shown him all the ropes, I talked for the last time to my Staff. I thanked them all for the happy times we had had together, and went on to give them a final word of advice: 'I know you all too well to qualify in any way my advice for the future. We have discussed together many, many times the probable future of our country and you know that in all probability it will be run, *de facto* or *de jure*, by the Russians. If you survive, which I sincerely hope you will, do not hesitate to join the Communist Party. You will be thus able to do quite a lot of good. Remember, Stalin is not eternal. Nor is communism.'

I then said my farewells and went to report to Tench. This meeting again changed my fate. It lasted for three days, during which Tench did most of the talking. He insisted that he was acting in an unofficial capacity, that he was talking to me as an older and wiser man with many responsibilities. He begged me not to accept the command offered me and act instead as his Chief of Staff, as it were, helping him to organize all the forces for the now imminent STORM. He said that he perfectly understood my feelings about my new command; he would stress, however, that more important tasks would have to be tackled in the near future. STORM would involve the unification of all the partisan groups now existing, and the mobilization of all the forces in the two Districts. Coordination, communications and logistic problems existed which he, Tench, would not be able to solve by himself and he could not see anyone around who could help him to do the job efficiently. Would I agree? For the sake of the Cause? Forgetting all personal ambitions? Tench himself would use what influence he had to change my orders.

For three days Tench went on and on in this vein. I could see very well that he was right. He would never be able to put everything together. He knew too few people and, in some respects, was like a child lost in a fog. My feelings were mixed. On the one hand I had a feeling that unfair pressure was being exerted on me, requiring me to abandon all expectations of 'glory' and all my dreams. On the other hand, I thought that this was the moment when I had to live up to my convictions and to practice what I had preached, i.e., that in an ideological war there should be no place for personal feelings of any sort, or for any thought of an explicit, or implicit, reward.

Towards the evening of the third day I said, 'All right.'

I contacted Mruk and told him to carry on as before, except that Mruk would be now under Tench's direct orders. I established my new headquarters at the home of the cousin with whom my wife had stayed for one winter. Since much paperwork was involved in my new job, I also had to organize strict security. In my room I had quite an arsenal: a machine-pistol, my Wis and a few hand grenades. The whole household was involved in my work and my cousin's wife, Anna, acted as my courier.

One day in early July a terrific explosion in the sky shattered the windows of the house. Inside the hour the whole area was saturated with German forces, combing the countryside and leaving no stone unturned. The next day my people reported that some metal debris had been found near Ozarow. The debris included what looked like a complicated electro-mechanical device. They were told to hide it until Warsaw could be notified, and then to deliver it to a special courier who would come to fetch it. Two days later the device was in Warsaw. I believe that it was part of a rocket, the firing range of which was near Mielec in the south.

XII

In the Open

EVENTUALLY, THE long-awaited 24 July came. The recent attempt on Hitler's life had put the German administration into disarray. Their armies were retreating on all fronts and in the east were falling back on the River Vistula. The BBC broadcasts began to play the tune 'With the smoke of fires'. STORM was under way.

All the forces from the Opatow and Sandomierz Districts had received orders to gather on the 24th at a forester's hut near Wlostow, south of Opatow and west of the Opatow—Sandomierz road. Tench was already there, and all forces had received the appropriate orders to join him. I had to join Tench during the afternoon.

But there were difficulties. The countryside was thick with Tartars of the Vlasov army.* Since everyone living at my cousin's house spoke Russian, they behaved roughly but correctly. They were, however, looking for and confiscating any available horses. They had not found any because all the cattle and horses were hidden in the deep ravines around the estate. I gathered up all my papers, maps and arms and went to look for the groom. My mare was not a saddle horse and with my cousin's agreement I swapped her for a stallion called Hucul, half Don Cossack and half Carpathian Highlander, a

---

* A force raised by the Germans from Russian PoWs and commanded by the captured Soviet General Vlasov.

small horse, black as night, reared by hand, docile as a child and as sure-footed as a mountain goat. Off I went on the stallion, choosing footpaths and barely visible tracks. We were shot at by Tartars only once; they could not follow us in the rough country and soon abandoned the chase. At full gallop we jumped across the Opatow–Sandomierz road and a few hundred metres beyond we met our first Partisan sentry. We were safe for the time being.

There were three of us: Tench, Mole, the security officer from the Sandomierz District (a few weeks earlier I had been a witness at his marriage to one of the girl couriers and had had to sign the register with my proper name), and I. We were guarded by Mruk and his fifty men. We had plenty of food and drink to keep us supplied while we waited for all the dispersed groups to get together, ultimately to form the 2nd Division of the Home Army. There were delays. One company from Sandomierz had been surrounded and annihilated. Andy's company was involved in a running battle with the German forces. Near Staszow his men had liquidated the Staff of the Pioneers of the IVth Panzer Armée. Documents seized in this skirmish showed an amazing likeness to the German ODB as established by the Home Army Intelligence. Intelligence personnel had, however, begun to suffer casualties. One of the observers of German Army movements was seen by the Field Gendarmerie to make notes while an armoured column was passing and was arrested and shot on the spot. Observing German movements became more difficult. They suddenly became wary of navvies, of farmers working near the roads, of shepherds and even of women putting out their washing. Identity checks and searches were carried out on all roads. The result was that about a dozen people were summarily convicted and shot as spies. The Russians were approaching the right bank of the Vistula and the fight for the bridgehead at Baranow, opposite Staszow, had begun.

Tench had decided to move further west, beyond the Opatow–Staszow road, in the territory of the 'Rakow

129

Republic', where the Germans had not as yet dared to venture. Tench established his command post at Szumsko, one of the local manors, where he intended to wait for the concentration of his forces to be completed.

I used the lull to send an armed escort to fetch Irena and Andrew from Opatow, which I thought would be in the direct line of the Russian assault, and to move them into the 'Rakow Republic'. I went to meet them. Irena was somewhat shaken and the escort reported two horses destroyed. What had happened was that while she was packing their few belongings, Andrew had found a Sten gun and, when Irena was at the back of the cart putting something into it, Andrew pressed the trigger. The first bullet went through Irena's coat under her right armpit, then the Sten jumped to the right and, before Andrew threw the gun down in terror, four more bullets missed Irena on her left side and shattered the legs of two horses standing behind her.

The ladies—Irena, Tench's wife and the wife of Major Wiktorowski, C.O. of the 2nd Regiment—stayed for a few days.

The troop concentration ended with the arrival of the 3rd Battalion of the 2nd Infantry Regiment. The Battalion had made contact with the Russians near Staszow and had taken part with them in the assault and the capture of this town.

On 2 August we heard on the news that Warsaw had risen in arms against the Germans. Until then I had hoped against hope that the High Command would postpone this confrontation. True, for the last days of July we could hear Moscow Radio calling for Warsaw to rise against the 'common enemy'. We heard that the Red Army was advancing on the whole of the Eastern front and that it was our duty to give it help. I hoped that we would wait and see. After all, it would mainly be a political decision and the National Government in Warsaw surely would remember all too well what had happened in 1939, what had happened at Katyn. They must know, and indeed they did, about the mass executions of the officers of the Vilno and Volyn divisions. They must know about the establishment of the co-called Lublin Committee in July, a committee in direct opposition to the legal Polish government in London. I had a feeling that the Russians would not help Warsaw, that they would let the Germans crush the uprising and let them do the dirty work of getting rid of the thousands of men and women with drive, initiative and qualities of leadership. If only Hitler had some imagination, I thought, and ordered his troops to surrender the city to the Home Army, he would gain six months, perhaps more. The Soviet Army would then have to stop at the River Vistula. They would not dare to move west, leaving behind them an armed city of about two million people, full of energy after the liberation and in constant radio contact with London and thereby with the whole world. Unfortunately Hitler was stupid and ordered his army to suppress the uprising.

True, there was another problem, and that was the problem of containing the accumulated hatred of the people who had suffered so heavily over the past six years. But, I thought, the Home Army is an *army* and what sort of commanding officer is it who cannot expect a direct order to be obeyed?

My hope was in vain. Warsaw had risen and we were supposed to go to its aid. But we began to have problems of our own and the Warsaw uprising became, in due course, of only secondary importance to us.

On 4 August, 1944 the first Russian T34 rumbled by the manor house. Behind them came the armoured personnel carriers, communication carriers and AA guns. It was the spearhead of the 117th Armoured Stalin Guards Brigade. Contact with the Russians was established. Meeting the Russian front-line troops was like meeting comrades-in-arms fighting the same enemy and for the same cause.

Although the Russians were somewhat condescending, they were friendly and willing to talk about the fighting. They availed themselves of the opportunity to use our reliable intelligence reports, which identified for them not only the strength and the disposition of the enemy forces but also their composition, morale, average age, armament and strong points. Together we probed the German forces north of the Opatow–Kielce road. There were virtually no casualties on the Home Army side but the Germans suffered heavily in every encounter.

However, when one began to touch on subjects other than military, an invisible wall would rise between the two parties. The Russians seemed neither to understand, nor to wish to understand, any question or problem other than military.

Except for the tanks, all the heavy equipment was American, visibly stamped U.S.A. The Russian explanation was invariably that they had stamped it so because the same equipment was being shipped to the United States to help the war effort of their great Allies. It was no use trying to convince them that it was actually the other way round.

After the armour, the infantry. They came like lice, a mass of men moving on foot, covering every road, every track, every path in the countryside. And with the infantry and the rear echelons, came the *Politruki*, the Political Commissars and the NKVD. With their arrival the atmosphere began to change radically. The soldiers stopped talking altogether. The commissars now did all the talking and only discussed politics at that. During every rest, at every meal, at every encounter of a group of Home Army men, the commissars tried to assess the morale of the Home Army and its political beliefs, insisting always that the Home Army submit to their military and political authority. Arms, decorations and promotions were being offered in profusion in an effort to draw the men from the Home Army and send them to enrol under the command of General Berling, in command of those Polish divisions fighting under the Russians.

I did my best to provoke them every time I had the opportunity to talk to them. They were all alike, however, and, as one would expect, they never talked freely. One day,

132

while out on a walk, I met a solitary Russian Captain sitting, dead drunk, on a tree stump.

'Hello, my lucky friend,' the Captain said in Russian. His speech was very slurred.

'Hello to you too,' I answered, also in Russian. 'But why lucky?'

'Because you are you and not me. Do you know my rank before I was demoted to Captain for drunkenness?'

'No, what was it?'

'I was a Colonel in the NKVD. Do you know what NKVD is?'

'I know,' I said. 'But the police exist in every civilized country,' I added teasingly.

'S . . t,' replied the Captain. 'Civilization, law and order—what are you talking about? I will tell you something. I was born the son of a kulak [a well-to-do peasant]. My family was liquidated in the purge of 1927. I was brought up at a special school. I worked hard. I did well. I was loyal, and progressed. I was made a member of the Party. I loved my country. I rose to the rank of Major and then Colonel in the NKVD. As a Colonel I had access to the library of Western books, though even I had to have a special pass. And there, in the quiet of the library, I was able to think, to think on my own, to use my own judgement on what I read. It makes you throw up when you hear all their propaganda. They corrupt everyone and everything. They are liars. Hitler said that the greater the lie the more likely people will believe in it; but your people know, if only subconsciously, what is the truth and what is a lie. We do not know the difference any more. Only lies exist and we cannot see truth of any kind.'

'Who are these "they" you talk about?' I asked.

'Who? This s.o.b. bastard, "Batiushka" Stalin and his clique. It makes you vomit when you think about this s . . .'

'Aren't you afraid to talk to a perfect stranger like this? You must usually be wary of strangers, mustn't you?'

'I am not afraid to talk to you because I like you,' he

133

answered with a drunkard's conviction. 'And I do not give a damn whether you betray me or not. I know that my days are numbered. Do you know that I have already survived a spell in the penal battalion of our brigade? The Great Patriotic War, and we have to have penal battalions. They are nothing else but execution squads in reverse, as it were. You attack the German position at an even pace, in an upright posture. If you keep upright you are mown down by the Germans; if you bend you are mown down by the special squads of NKVD from behind. You die a hero. Nobody would dare to point out that your body had been riddled by bullets from behind. Yet I continue to fight because I love my country.'

'So do I,' I said. 'In this respect we are allies, aren't we?'

'Allies? Yes, perhaps, but only because the West has double standards. To win the war you would make the Devil your ally, explaining to the world that the Devil could, after all, be reformed by gentleness, good will and persuasion. And indeed, the Devil, or our Batiushka, seems to be so. But remember, my friend, that the West will pay in blood and toil for years as the price of this pact. Your Roosevelt must be mad to make such an agreement as Yalta. Your Churchill is less gullible perhaps, but has not guts and not enough strength to say no. History will demonstrate their madness, or naivety, in political matters. After all, a politician, or a leader, can overcome all criticism except that of stupidity. Have you seen our equipment? Except for the tanks, it is all American. Your Allies have unprecedented military power, a power which has never even been approached in history. They could do it on their own, and yet, using the double standard of morality and perverting the meaning of the word democracy, you made these bastards a great democratic ally and you will thus sell into slavery Latvia, Estonia, Lithuania, Poland, Czecho-slovakia, Romania, Bulgaria, Yugoslavia and, in the long run, I do not know how many other countries of the world. It makes you throw up. You say that Hitler is a genocidal maniac. S . . t. He couldn't hold a candle to our Batiushka.

134

Hitler is simply an inept pupil. Forgetting all the purges which used to take place in my country one after another, do you know that in 1937 Krushchev, on the orders of our Batiushka, managed to liquidate twelve million Ukranians? What Hitler has managed to achieve is just chickenfeed. And we still have to forget all of it, to fight and to die.'

His voice was beginning to fade.

'For what? For whom?' He shuddered and went to sleep.

Two days later, leading a patrol, I found his body, along with two others, shot. By whom? I did not know, and had no opportunity to investigate. Too many Russians were about.

The situation was becoming more and more difficult and precarious. Friendly discussions had now developed into political harangues. Veiled threats of force were becoming frequent. The front-line soldiers abandoned their initial comradely attitude. The *Politruks*, knowing nothing of the existence of Tench, were clamouring to meet Raven (Major Krukowski), the C.O. of the 2nd Regiment. In the wake of the Russian advance, the survivors of the Home Army groups to the east of the Vistula had started to filter back and join the 2nd Division. All of them brought the same news. There were two major partisan groups of the Home Army to the east of the country: the Vilno Division and the Volyhnian Division. After surrendering to the Russians, on orders from London, they were all disarmed. The other ranks were then immediately sent to Russia and the officers, after being ordered to attend a supposed staff meeting, were massacred. All independent groups fighting the Germans were being hunted down and liquidated. Katyn was being perpetrated on various scales all over again. News began to reach Tench of the arrest of members of the Home Army and of civilians in the 'liberated' parts of the district. No orders from Kielce were forthcoming. Delaying tactics had to be adopted.

On my instigation Tench issued orders to all his forces to break away from the Russians, then instructed them, after crossing the German lines, to go to the rescue of Warsaw where the insurrection had now been going on for several days. True, the Russians were held up at this stage because of logistic problems. Their artillery had only two rounds of ammunition left per piece and although the infantry was living off the land (their iron rations consisted of some *Kasha* (groats) and some pork fat), there was an evident shortage of fuel and obvious difficulties in bringing any ammunition up to the front. Nevertheless, the idea of going to the rescue of Warsaw was preposterous. Warsaw was about a hundred and twenty kilometres away. To reach it we would have to break through twelve fortified German lines of defence, advancing across open country with the Hermann Goering Panzer Division reported to be moving in from the west. While agreeing with the idea of breaking off from the Russians, I tried in vain to dissuade Tench from going on towards Warsaw. He explained to me one evening in private that this was just a ploy to avoid any questions from the rank and file about the necessity for such a move.

By that time, probably because of my critical attitude, Tench's Staff was gradually being taken over by infantry men—Major Raven (Kruk), Lieutenants Mole (Kret) and Grey (Siwy). Most of the time I was now spending on guard duty with my fifty men.

The final rendezvous before crossing the Holy Cross Mountains was fixed for 1600 hrs at a forester's hut south of the Opatow–Kielce road, with the final briefing of all the C.O.s at 1800 hours. During the briefing the sentries reported that a Russian Major had come to see Raven. Tench retired into a spare room. The Major came in, listened for some time, and left, saying that he would be back. An hour later he reappeared with a message from the Russian Divisional Commander inviting all the officers of the 2nd Division of the Home Army to attend a special meeting at the Russian Divisional Command Post. So that was their idea. Raven and I went to report to Tench. The old pattern of treachery was now in evidence. As expected, Tench decided that only Raven should go and should make any necessary excuses for refusing to join the Russians and submit to their command.

Raven asked me to accompany him. Together it would be easier for us to wriggle out of the situation and my presence would boost his morale. He had to admit that it was not at its highest. I do not know why, but I agreed. After all, I spoke Russian fluently and knew something about them. We decided to take our runners with us. All were armed with sub-machine-guns. We mounted our horses and, with the Russian Major, entered the forest. Immediately we were surrounded by at least a platoon of Russian cavalry.

At about 1930 hours we arrived at the Command Post of the Divisional Commander. Two officers met us. Both were in Russian field brown uniform, both Colonels, with NKVD flashes on their collars. They apologized profusely for the fact that the Divisional Commander could not attend the meeting owing to pressure of other work. They had been authorized to speak in his name. They introduced themselves as *Politruks* of the Division. The older, a tall, stout Jew, mentioned that he was from Bialystok (a town in the north-east of Poland). The younger said that he was a descendant of a Polish family in the Ukraine. He came from Kharkov.

At once they asked Raven why it was that the other officers of the Division he commanded had not come with him. Raven explained that his officers had to stay with their respective commands, the Division having received orders to move over to the German side of the front. The Russians did not like this at all.

One of the runners sat behind me and Raven's runner stood under a tree nearby. Light was provided by a candle stuck in the neck of an empty bottle. On the fringe of the dim light it cast, armed men could be seen moving around like ghosts. We were offered vodka. Raven refused very politely, saying that we were not used to drinking when on duty—a blatant lie, but one the Russians had to swallow. Cigarettes were then passed around. Their high quality and their availability and low price

137

in Russia were mentioned. Raven and I were suitably impresssed.

The conversation kept to the typical interrogation pattern of the NKVD. The elder of the two Russians was trying to pump us about the essentials: what were our numbers, equipment, ammunition, morale? What was the predominant social class of all other ranks? What means of communications had we? At what time did we communicate with the outside world and with whom? Every few minutes he would pause and then the younger Colonel would start to interject some purely military questions about the Germans, their order of battle, their morale, their strength. He would interpolate reminiscences about common actions, enemy losses and the like. This continuous switching from fundamentals to trivia was quite exhausting. It was left to me to answer the questions put by the older Colonel. When the going became too difficult it was Raven's turn to enlarge enthusiastically, in the manner of the younger one, on the merits, the bravery, etc, etc of the soldiers of their ally. According to Raven, it was the Poles who had made it possible for the bridgehead at Baranow to be established. Raven was so blatantly flannelling the Russians that even they seemed sometimes to be at a loss as to whether to be angry or to let it pass.

So far I was coping quite well; I knew what the supply situation of the Russian army was; I could make, and was making, the strength of the Home Army appear much greater than it was in reality. With great aplomb I told them that, from many air drops, the Home Army was very well equipped with the PIAT anti-tank weapon. I told them that the officers and other ranks all belonged to the working or peasant class; that their morale was of the highest; that all were ready to obey any order given to them by their superiors.

'As you may have seen for yourselves when we were fighting together for Staszow,' chipped in Raven.

We implied that every battalion was in direct contact with Raven, who in his turn was in direct contact with London four

138

times a day. (Actually the contact was an indirect once, via the Dawn (Jutrzenka) station somewhere in Sweden).

Eventually the older Colonel put the following question: 'What is the disposition of your forces?'

Here Raven excelled himself. He took out of his pouch a 1:250,000 map, put his palm with spread fingers across it and said, 'Here.'

For a moment I thought that Raven had overdone it. The NKVD men looked at each other for a long time. Then, evidently deciding to overlook this stupid statement by a semi-literate Pole, they changed their tactics.

'Would you be willing to recognize the Lublin Committee?' asked the older Colonel. 'After all, this is now the only Polish government truly representative of the masses.'

'We do not know anything about this Committee. We obey orders from the Polish Government in London.'

'But you had orders to fight side by side with us. How can you do it without being members of General Berling's Polish Army, which is under our command?'

'But these orders have now been superseded by an order to go to the rescue of Warsaw, which you are not doing, nor are you able to.' I answered.

A plane droned overhead. All the lights went out. I wanted to pull my boot up. A torch at once shone on my hands.

The Russians now produced a huge poster with twelve photographs of the members of the Lublin Committee.

'Do you know who he is? And he?' and so on.

'We do not know any of them,' I said. 'But just a moment. I think I know one of them. He looks like one of the inmates of the Holy Cross prison. I hope that I am wrong.'

They went back to trying to persuade us to join Berling. Again and again my answer was: 'We cannot; we have our orders; we are only soldiers and we must go to the aid of Warsaw.'

Again the same arguments. If we accepted Raven would be promoted to the rank of Colonel and given a regiment to

139

command. They knew that I was a Lieutenant-Commander. It was therefore suggested that surely in the 'Free' Polish Forces a rank of Commander or even higher could be found for me.

All the time the answers were the same: we are under the orders of the Polish Government in London; we are soldiers; we obey orders; we cannot decide on our own. On and on it went in this vein. The tension was becoming unbearable. Eventually one last question was put in a sharp tone to Raven and me:

'And if we give you an explicit order to join us, what will you do?'

'We have our orders. And if you do not mind, we have to leave you now. We have to join our men, who are already on the move.'

A heavy silence fell, broken only by the occasional explosions of German heavy artillery shells in the distance. The corner of my eye caught the slight movement of my runner's hand towards the safety-catch of his Sten. My own fingers moved delicately towards the safety catch of my Udet, sliding it into the firing position. If we have to go, I thought, at least the two of them will go first.

The two NKVD men looked at each other in silence for what seemed like an eternity. Eventually the older one said, '*Nu, chtozh. Puskay yedut* (Well, let them go).'

We all shook hands and said a very formal goodbye. I had trouble with my legs. For the first time in my life they seemed to be made of cotton wool. Eventually I managed to stand up and we mounted our horses; then, unaccompanied this time by the Russians, we galloped into the darkness of the forest.

At 11 pm we rejoined our men, now on the move over one of the more inaccessible mountain passes, cut deep into the rock. I was glad to have a mountain horse under me. In the pitch dark, on the road strewn with stones and boulders and pitted with pot-holes, my horse walked as boldly and as easily as on a smooth highway. On the top of the pass I turned

140

round. Before me was the Sandomierz Plateau. It was on fire. Houses, hay-stacks, woods were burning everywhere. And they would burn for months to come.

By morning we were through to the other side of the mountain range. We stopped for a day at a village at the foot of the mountains. In the evening I led a reconnaissance party. It was pitch dark. As we moved along in silence we heard horses. It was a Vlasov cavalry patrol, as we later learned. One good volley and they fled. After a few minutes tanks and infantry began to move in. I retreated. I reported the movement of the German armour and infantry to Tench and an hour later the Division was again on the move, towards the west, skirting the foot of the mountain range all the time. In the dark we nearly shot up a patrol from the Kielce District, but fortunately there were no casualties.

The next day Tench stopped at a forester's hut. I was with him when four officers entered with an ultimatum: all should go to the rescue of Warsaw. I had to admire Tench on this occasion. He pretended not to see the drawn pistols, flatly said no and then explained why: too many Germans, open country with no possible shelter and twelve fortified German lines, ready to meet the Russian advance. The officers did not know quite what to do. They looked at each other, then at Tench, then at me and my Udet at the ready. Eventually they said that they understood the situation and retired. That was the first hint of dissatisfaction among the officers and their men. It was understandable. For two days now they had done nothing but march. They wanted action. Little did they know that they would soon have plenty of it.

The same night we crossed the Radom—Kielce road, encountering on our way a number of tanks and troop carriers moving south. The fireworks were fantastic. The PIATs stopped the three leading tanks, which started to burn after exploding. Heavy machine-gun fire prevented German deployment. The tracers were virtually making night into day. Surprisingly we managed to cross the road without any casualties and went up the hill into a dense forest, pursued ineffectively by shells and by tracer from the German column. The staff went to rest in a forest clearing covered with surprisingly large bushes of bilberries as large as damsons. Very soon all uniforms, where there were any, had acquired a nice camouflage of large, darkish stains.

We moved off in the evening, entering the country with prominently displayed signposts reading: '*Achtung. Banditen*'.

It was the Konskie District, where Grey had been taking a heavy toll of Germans for the last two months. At night we met a large group of the Russian-led 'People's Army' and Tench had again to refuse to join them. In the next two days we engaged the Germans on three separate occasions. The first encounter was with a billetting party for the Staff of the IVth Panzer Armée. All were killed and a beautiful eight-cylinder Horch belonging to their Chief of Staff was captured undamaged and brought to the Command Post.

In the second encounter Andy's battalion engaged some Germans on a punitive expedition to one of the villages, led by the Gestapo Chief from the town of Lublin. The German force consisted of Vlasov's Kalmuks and the Gendarmerie, travelling in about twenty lorries, the Gestapo men in staff cars. Very soon all the staff cars were on fire and the main German force was scurrying in haste towards the lorries and leaving the village. The Gestapo men, twelve in all, were trapped in a ditch. They refused to surrender and, after a fierce fight, they were finished off with hand grenades. While this was going on, Andy's men had laid down an ambush for the retreating lorries. The mainstay of the ambush was Charles, a Frenchman from Alsace, who was a master at working an MG 43 (Spandau). He was helped by a further five machine-guns, all hidden in the trees some fifty yards from the road. When the lorries appeared, going at full speed, the machine-guns opened up. It was a massacre. The road was soon strewn with burning lorries and the troops trying to escape were mowed down relentlessly by Charles. Charles was very soon firing alone, his companions just looking on admiringly at his precision, as he unerringly picked off every single moving German. The ambush had to retire on the approach of a large German force supported by tanks, coming from the direction of Konskie. Subsequent intelligence reports confirmed the complete annihilation of the punitive force.

The third action took place the next day, when a strong patrol engaged a German forced-labour recruiting party. The Germans were rounding up all the men in another village and shooting down all who tried to escape, including women and children. The party consisted of about twenty Gendarmes, with two civilians in charge. After a short exchange of fire the Gendarmes fled, leaving behind a few dead, and the two civilians, very frightened but unharmed.

The two civilians were brought to me. Both had had their clothes removed and stood in their underwear, their hands tied behind their backs. The older one, in charge of the expedition, was a certain Herr Lindt, a Nazi Party member, his card bearing the number 13, a very low number, but very unlucky for him. He was arrogant during interrogation and broke down only when his escort was told to take him and his henchman into the forest and to shoot both of them. I again had the experience of seeing a man who did not hesitate to shoot innocent people, including women and children, break down and defecate in his underwear when going to share the fate he had meted out to so many others. The bodies were left in the forest to rot.

All this time I felt more and more estranged from Tench and from the new members of his Staff. At the same time I became every day closer to my horse. The animal was totally unmoved by the heaviest of firing. He was a firm favourite with all the men, who used to feed him by hand with apples, bread and whatever they had. By now he was as fat as a barrel and I was finding it difficult to prevent the saddle from slipping around his sleek body. While other horses were in difficulties because of the shortage of oats, my small stallion

143

could eat any quantity of barley without ill effect, enjoying it and constantly asking for more.

During the next few days the Division headed towards the now fortified range of hills near the town of Malogoszcz. We were in the thick of the German forces. On Sunday Tench established his headquarters in a hut in the woods near the Skarzysko–Konskie railway line. That Sunday proved to be another turning point in my life. I was growing closer and closer to the fifty men from my old District command. I always had a rough shelter prepared by them for the night and they always managed to provide me with food. That Sunday morning they came to me saying that the men were being denied access to the only source of fresh water in the woods, a well in the courtyard of the forester's hut where Tench was sleeping. They said, with some indignation, that when they wanted to draw some water from the well early in the morning, they were turned out of the courtyard by members of Tench's Staff. Tench could not be disturbed. He was asleep and it did not matter whether nor not the men were thirsty.

I went to see Tench. I had to wait. I did not feel at all happy. After all, there had been times when he had relied completely on me. It was I who had coached him in the rudiments of survival in territory overrun by Germans. It was I who, for three years, had taken care of his well-being, providing him with 'safe' houses and security. Now I had to await his pleasure before being admitted into his presence. I saw him at about 10 am. He was awake and ready for the day, having drunk his ration of half a bottle of moonshine.

I did not mince my words. I told him that it was inhuman and against all rules of leadership to let one's men go thirsty. He should not prevent men from drawing water, irrespective of whether he was asleep or not. Sooner or later such an attitude would be his undoing. In future I would not abide by any such orders issued by him. And that was that.

In reply Tench said that, because of my attitude, he could see no further need for me to stay with the force. He immediately ordered me to leave and return to Kielce, where I would have to report to the Regional Commander.

'This order is final,' said Tench. 'Goodbye.'

I saluted and left.

XIII

Alone

THE PARTING WITH my men made up for any disillusion I might have felt and restored my faith in human nature and in life in general. The men were moved; they were concerned. I had to shake fifty hands many, many times. Swallowing my tears, I fastened my rucksack and left.

I crossed the railway line and in the forester's house I met Dahlia and her cousin Maria of all people! They were making their way to Cracow since Dahlia's estate was too near the front line. I spent the night with them, and in the morning left my stallion with the forester and went on foot to a railway halt, hoping to catch any train going towards Skarzysko. At the halt I met two women, couriers from the C.O. in Kielce, returning home from Tench. During the night one of the fortified posts along the railway line had been smashed by Grey and we had to be prepared to meet Germans patrolling the track. We did indeed see a German patrol in the distance, and so we started to play cards. When the Germans approached they saw a man and two women engaged in a heated discussion over a game of three-handed bridge. The Germans were rather subdued. They demanded to see our documents and asked what we were doing. On learning that we were fleeing from the Russian advance, they went off.

A distant rumble came from the skies high above us: hundreds of condensation trails, American or British bombers going east.

The train came. It was going to Kielce, just where I had to go.

Leaving the station at Kielce I suddenly found myself beside Mrs M., in whose flat I had had my communication centre when I was the Signals Officer for the Kielce Province of the Home Army. I nearly said hello to her when I suddenly realized that on her other side was a Gestapo man whom I knew by sight. She walked past me without even looking at me and disappeared into the crowd. I thanked God. I could remember many occasions when, by acting against my inclinations, I had avoided confrontation. This time the confrontation would have been a final one. I was not armed and I could have done nothing if apprehended.

I met my contact and the next day saw the C.O. of the Province. He was a new man, appointed to the post a few months earlier. The old C.O. had been summoned to Warsaw, was arrested on his way to the capital and the news was that he had been shot immediately. The new C.O. did not know much about the situation, which was changing from day to day. He had orders, however, to organize an underground resistance movement against the communist Lublin Committee and against the Russians. In view of the official attitude of the Allies towards the Russians, an attitude also held by the Polish Government in London, this did not make much sense. Soon it also proved to be impractical. Not one of my old colleagues and none of my new contacts seemed interested in setting up a subversive network against the régime which was inevitably coming soon and coming to stay. The zest for conspiracy seemed to have disappeared. People had had enough of it; they were no longer sure of their feelings, but they knew that they had had enough of the hide-and-seek which they had played with the Germans for five long years. Warsaw had surrendered after six weeks of hopeless fighting and was being destroyed street by street, house by house, with fire and dynamite. The Germans were definitely losing the war, the Allies were on the borders of the Reich. Why start another war?

147

I felt foolish. My persuasive abilities seemed to have disappeared. News was coming in about the disbanding of Tench's forces. After several heavy encounters, ammunition was getting low and the autumn weather was beginning to take its toll of the lightly-clad men. It was the end, the end both of the surreptitious and the open fighting. I felt that I could do nothing more and decided to say goodbye to Kielce, to go and lie low in my old district and try to find Irena and Andrew.

I managed to catch a train made up of flat-bed trucks, packed with all sorts of refugees. On the way we were strafed by a single Soviet fighter plane. The silly pilot could clearly see that the train did not carry any tanks, or any military personnel, yet he made passes over the train time and time again. The plane was a Spitfire, with eight machine guns blazing away during every pass. I could not understand why I had not been hit. The floor of the truck was like a sieve, with several people strewn around it, dead. As usual, I felt that my time had not yet come.

I was first taken to stay at the palace of Prince D.-L. The Prince himself and his family were away (it was too near the front line), and the palace was the Command Post of the Commander of the Hungarian Division. The Hungarian Division was holding that part of the front and the Hungarians were rather in sympathy with the Poles. They did not ask any questions and were quite happy to help the Poles as much as they could. In November I moved to Jeleniec to stay with the Halpert family, who received me with open arms. I settled down with them, keeping a low profile, and waited. The front line was stabilized, running through the small town of Bogorya, where I knew Irena had gone to stay with Raven's wife. The only thing I could do was to pray to God for their safety and to wait.

STORM proved to be a disaster for my old Command. My successor had mobilized all his forces in the forest north of Starachowice and kept them there in one location for three

148

days, with the result that the Germans had time to surround them. Fortunately for the men, since the Warsaw uprising the Home Army had been treated as combatants and so was subject to the Geneva Convention. Everyone, except the District C.O., had been taken prisoner. The C.O. had not had time to join them!

During my stay at Jeleniec I had ample time to think about what was going on and to weigh up the results of the war. Poland and the other eastern European countries were definitely the losers, especially Poland. Caught between Hitler and Stalin, she was bound to lose. What was the use of trying to fight the Germans? The country was nearly all open plain, with enemies on both sides of the front line. How different it was for the French or the Belgians, for instance. Every railway line damaged, every bridge blown was helping the Allied advance. Where were the Allies in Poland? Only Churchill, perhaps, had any idea of the true nature of Stalin. Roosevelt was just an old, ill man and surely would be judged by history as the man who, having it in his power to establish a new order on this earth, had frittered it all away in the politically suicidal pacts of Teheran and Yalta.

STORM was, therefore, bound to fail. But the Warsaw uprising was indeed an act of folly. I wondered how the High Command of the Home Army would try to justify this apalling action. If only the Germans had been a different enemy! General Bor-Komorowski could then have leaked to the German High Command the notion that the German retreat from Warsaw would be bound to stop the Russian advance! They would have had to sort out all the political and military problems of leaving, behind their front lines, a city of nearly two million people, about 40,000 of them armed, and a well-organized army in hourly communication with the West. Surrendering Warsaw to the Poles would have stopped the Russian front at the Vistula for at least six months, perhaps more! Hitler, however, had no imagination; Warsaw was taken; the threat to the Russian rear disappeared and Stalin

149

could move forward! And the capital had been destroyed with untold human losses, leaving the rest of the Home Army without any command structure.

During my stay at Jeleniec something happened which made me even more disillusioned and which, in my estimation, vindicated both my inactivity and my semi-official retirement. As already mentioned, the front line near Ostrowiec was partly manned by the Hungarians. Throughout history Poland and Hungary have had very close ties. I now had an opportunity to observe them. They were good friends. They helped the starving from their own meagre rations; they were helpful with the transport of civilians and turned a blind eye to any subversive activity, not seeing armed men, not enquiring into the status of any lodger at their billets. If one wanted to cross over to the Russian side through their sector they would give any necessary help.

A young man appeared at Jeleniec. He quite openly said to Mr Halpert that for some time he had been attached to the High Command of the Home Army which, after the fall of Warsaw, had re-formed somewhere near Cracow. His name was Tabor and, according to his statement, he was the younger brother of General Tabor, who was in charge of Polish operations in London. He wanted to cross over to the Russian side. Only there, he claimed, could he be of some use. He asked for permission to stay and rest for a few days. Since at the time they had no free rooms at Jeleniec, he was sent to Baltow, Prince D.-L.'s palace. An hour after he had left two men from District Intelligence appeared and started to ask questions about young Tabor. Since they knew Mr Halpert, they confided in him that an execution squad from High Command was due in Ostrowiec with orders to liquidate the young man. He had to be killed because he knew the address of the Command Post of the Home Army near Cracow. Being a communist, or at least a communist sympathizer with the new Lublin régime, he was a danger to the staff of the Home Army.

I was shocked and furious. Here I was, deposed from my

command because I had to fight the communists to protect the lives of Home Army men. These lives did not seem to mean much to men playing politics. They were expendable. And now, when the same people appeared to be in possible personal danger, politics went overboard and they had no hesitation in giving orders to kill, knowing perfectly well that since the Russians had taken over the country's security services no hiding place could be found in Poland where they would be secure.

It took me two days to find the reluctant C.O. of the District and for two long hours I tried to persuade him of the fallacy of the proposed execution. The C.O. hedged, saying that it was not his decision, that he had to obey orders, and so on. Eventually I slammed the door behind me and rushed to Baltow to warn the young man. It was too late. An hour earlier he had been whisked away and shot a hundred yards from the house.

I suddenly felt very lonely and disspirited. The years of fighting, the years of effort, the years during which I felt I had found the heart of the people, their greatness and humility, all seemed to recede into a bleak, hopeless future. Nothing could be done except wait. But wait for what?

In the evening of 10 January, 1945, Jeleniec was full of German cavalry. At midnight they suddenly left. At 3 am on 11 January the picture hanging over my bed suddenly fell down. The whole house was shaking. I got up and went to the window. From it I could see well beyond Ostrowiec across the Plain of Sandomierz. From the foot of the Holy Cross Mountains to my right and stretching to the east, there was across the whole horizon a continuous band of fire—thousands of Russian guns delivering a heavy barrage. The Russian breakout from the Baranow bridgehead had started.

Early on Tuesday morning the news came that the Russians were in Ostrowiec. I had to make a decision. I knew that as soon as they found me it would be curtains for me and not very pleasant curtains at that. I also knew that the NKVD teams

151

would go west, following the advancing army, leaving behind skeleton NKVD cells to keep an eye on that part of the country already thoroughly cleared of all 'unreliable' elements. To survive, I must go east and hope to be able to live for a while undetected among the thousands of refugees, some returning to the east, some waiting to go to the west of the country. Then there were Irena and Andrew. My wife and my son had to be found. Only with Irena could I eventually make the final decision about what to do with our lives.

I armed myself with two bottles of vodka, the transport currency of the Russian Army, and on the afternoon of that Tuesday Mr Halpert took me in his carriage to the other end of Ostrowiec. On our way through the town we saw processions with red banners and slogans hailing Lenin, Stalin, the leaders of the Lublin Committee and the Prime Minister-designate of the new Warsaw government. It was all very professionally organized, following the pattern of the old Russian Revolution.

I said goodbye to Mr Halpert at the crossroads and half an hour later I thumbed a lift in an army lorry to Opatow; by waving a half-litre of vodka.

The town was in ruins and nearly empty of inhabitants. I managed to find, nevertheless, some old friends, cousins of Roman. They received me with open arms. We ate together and talked well into the night. Roman had already disappeared. The arrests had started to take place within an hour of the Russian arrival. The two men were old and hoped that they would be left alone.

The next morning, again with the help of a bottle of vodka, I reached Sandomierz, where I hoped to find my Ukrainian cousin.

Only his mother-in-law was at their flat. He and the rest of the family had been evacuated to a smallholding in a village near the town of Tarnobrzeg, on the east bank of the Vistula. To cross the river one had to have a special pass from the NKVD, which was not good news.

The prospects for my survival were somewhat dubious. I was completely 'blown'. Whenever I went out people approached me in the streets offering me shelter and help. Young men saluted me, whom I vaguely recognized as members of the 2nd Division. I asked one of them to go to Bogorya to enquire about Irena. The next day he was back with the news that Irena and Andrew were safe and well, but that Irena was already on her way to Ostrowiec to look for me. The young man had left a note saying that I was waiting for her at such and such an address. There was nothing else for me to do but to wait.

I also tried to find a way to cross the river without going to the NKVD to get a pass to cross the only bridge. I was lucky. In the street I met the old Medical Officer of the District, who had been evacuated to Sandomierz. His sister-in-law, a beautiful woman who liked good living, was very friendly with the town's NKVD chief. She had a permanent permit from him to cross the bridge accompanied by her coachman. The coachman's name was not shown on the permit. A week after my arrival at Sandomierz I became a coachman and crossed the river without any trouble. We timed the crossing in such a way that the return journey by the lady alone would be after the changing of the guard at the bridge, so no questions would be asked about the whereabouts of the driver.

The same evening I was warmly greeted by my cousin and, as a matter of course, was invited to stay with the family. It was a perfect hiding place. All the outbuildings were used as stores for the Medical Supply Centre of Marshal Koniev's 3rd Ukrainian Army. The centre was under the command of a certain Major Sinichkin, with Lieutenant Bakhtadze, a Georgian, as his deputy.

The major, the son of a peasant from the Volga region, was an atheist and a dedicated communist with a surprisingly developed sense of humour. He did not mind, for instance, when my cousin, a man with quite a sharp tongue, addressed him and his deputy as 'Zolotopogonniki', the 'golden epaulets

153

men'. The discussions were interminable, the two parties disagreeing all the time and all the time agreeing to disagree.

Staying with us was my uncle Borys, an ex-Imperial Guard Officer, decorated twice during the First War with the highest military order of St George. Although he drank heavily, he was always full of initiative and he suggested to me that we should do some trading. He had already done some in the eastern part of the country and had all the necessary contacts about one hundred miles further east. We therefore bought about ten kilos of tobacco leaves and off we went in a farm cart driven by a pair of horses. We took to the secondary roads, avoiding the main ones which carried the heavy military traffic. The ride was quite an experience. Villages on our way were either completely destroyed or were standing untouched. The woods and the forest were devastated either by gunfire or by the felling of trees for bunkers. The countryside was empty of any wild life; no hares, no rabbits, no birds, nothing. All were shot, or had flown or scampered away. Not even a dog could be seen. They had all been taken by the Russians to be trained as mine sniffers, or to act as anti-tank mine carriers.

We sold the tobacco leaves and bought a half-side of pork with a thick layer of back fat. We were back within a week. From my portion I kept a few kilos of fat for myself; the rest I sold, and from the proceeds I could buy fifty American dollars on the black market. Quite a scoop.

In March Major Sinichkin and his team moved forward and Irena came to Sandomierz.

XIV

Irena at the Front

WHEN, IN JULY, I had sent Irena and Andrew to stay with Raven's wife near Bogorya, I thought that they would be away from the fighting. This small town was tucked away from all the main roads, and even the Germans during the occupation had seemed to avoid it. It was situated in territory in which Andy and his men had been operating since 1943. The best ideas are, however, sometimes thwarted by fate. Bogorya was directly in the line of the Russian advance from the Baranow bridgehead. When the 2nd Home Army Division left the region, the fight for Bogorya started. During the next two weeks it changed hands six times. Every time it underwent a severe bombardment from one side or the other. Irena, Andrew and several other women spent the whole two weeks in the cellar of a house, the top floors of which were hit several times by artillery fire. There was very little to eat and practically no fresh water. After two weeks, when the Germans had finally retreated, they emerged unscathed from the cellar. Irena and Andrew then went to live at the house of Raven's wife. The house was a billet for the Russian troops and a curious relationship developed between Irena and the Russians.

She cooked for the troops and thus had food for herself and her son. Andrew was a favourite of the older men. He reminded them of their own sons. They were all infantrymen and had virtually no medical services at all. Very soon soldiers started to come to Irena asking her to help them with their illnesses, especially dysentery, which was rife among the Russian troops. She became a great success among the Russians. She achieved this by making them drink a weak solution of potassium permanganate, of which she had a jar and which she was using as a disinfectant. She had some thread and used to darn their socks, sew on their buttons, help them with bandages, and so on. Very soon the Russians used to say to newcomers, 'Go and see Mrs Szymanska. She has everything.' She was never, at that time, threatened with rape, though a Captain propositioned her, offering her a sack of sugar if she would join him in bed. He could not understand why she would not agree. 'Why not? I am a member of your allied armed forces. You are a woman, your husband is away. You must need a man, and here I am', was his argument.

In January, 1945, the troops moved away and harder times began to loom ahead. Nevertheless, remembering 1939 and expecting similar shortages, Irena managed to fill one suitcase with soap which she had made herself, matches and some raw knitting wool, which she had obtained a few years back from my cousin.

Eventually there came a time when there was no more soap, no matches, no wool. Irena had to take measures in order not to starve. She started to smuggle tobacco leaves to Lublin, the seat of the new Warsaw government, selling the leaves on the black market and buying food to take back.

The only means of transport were, as usual, the Russian lorries. On every trip Irena had to defend herself against rape (luckily she was a very strong woman). Sometimes she had to explain to the drivers or soldiers that, although she recognized them as allies, this did not automatically mean that she had to make herself available to them. As a result of her resisting all attempts on several occasions she was thrown out of the lorry and had to walk several miles in severe weather to get back to Andrew. Very often she was hungry; she had blisters on her

156

feet and often had to sleep rough. But she overcame all this and survived.

February, 1945, came; the front receded to the west and she decided to go in search of her husband. She left Andrew in the care of a good woman, put on as much warm clothing as she could find and off she went, heading for Ostrowiec, some twenty miles away. She had to go over ice-bound roads and through fields treacherous with snowdrifts. Once she heard an explosion. She came upon a woman in a state of shock, her dead son's head cradled in her hands. They were in a mine-field. She had to go on and managed to get through safely. Having made enquiries at Ostrowiec she learned that I had gone east (I thought that I had covered my tracks quite well). She then went back to Bogorya and found my message. She packed whatever was left to pack and managed, with Andrew, to reach Sandomierz and get to my cousin's flat. The flat had by then been taken as a billet for the troops. Again she had to cook for the Russians and again she had sufficient to eat until the day when I went to fetch her and Andrew to take them across the river.

We stayed at my cousin's for two weeks. Then Irena and I decided to move to Tarnobrzeg. Major Sinichkin left and my cousin's fate was again becoming uncertain. When I left him in July, 1944, to join STORM I had drawn up and signed with my pseudonym a certificate in which, as the C.O. of the Opatow District of the Home Army, I certified that my cousin, although a Ukrainian, had not only behaved very properly during the German occupation but had taken an active part in the Resistance and had helped the Movement in any way he could. He was arrested the very day the Russians arrived, taken to the NKVD Headquarters, interrogated and released next day after he had produced my bit of paper. By that time I already knew that I had been sentenced to death. I knew that Mruk had been arrested, tortured and killed in a shocking manner. Yet the same people who had branded me as a perpetrator of fratricide were willing to honour my statement that somebody had behaved in an impeccable manner during the occupation! No logic in all this, but a lot of prevarication! Nevertheless, my cousin was expecting the NKVD or the new Polish security forces to arrest him again at any time. He thought that the first arrest and the subsequent release were a freak.

After looking around the town, I found a vacant room in one of the houses on the outskirts, from which the C.O. of the Tarnobrzeg District of the Home Army had been taken away by the NKVD. The room had a kitchen range, a table, one large and one small bed. We received a nanny goat as a present and, in April, 1945, Irena, Andrew and I moved into the house.

XV

The Teaching Days

As soon as we had all moved to Tarnobrzeg I started to look for a job. First of all I established contacts with the remnants of the Home Army personnel in the town. I was again lucky because my main contact was the intelligence officer of the District, a sergeant-major of the late Polish Army, well thought of by the authorities in the town. After consulting him, I decided that the most suitable job for me would be teaching. Communists and Russians respect the profession and it could provide me with decent cover, at least for a time.

First I went to see the director of the secondary school in the town, offering my services as a teacher of French, English, physics and mathematics. Although I could not produce any documents as to my education and qualifications, the Director seemed to be quite impressed, said that he would think about my application and told me to come back the next day. When he opened the door of his study five young men waiting in the corridor suddenly stood to attention on seeing me and saluted smartly. The Director looked at the young men, then at me, smiled and said, 'It seems to me that it would be of advantage to all of us if you would try to obtain a teaching post somewhere else.' I knew that he was right. We shook hands and I left.

There was, at the outskirts of the town, a newly-opened Agricultural College. The College was in the castle of Count

159

Tarnowski, a family associated with the town for centuries. I went to see the Director. They were so short of staff that the Director, without as much as looking at me, engaged me on the spot to teach English, physics and mathematics. The salary was nominal but was supplemented by a hundred kilos of wheat a month. I gladly accepted. On top of everything I could avoid the town when going to work.

And so the following week I started teaching, although I had to resign myself to the fact that, among my class of thirty five of the students had been with me during my spell with the 2nd Division. A sixth student was the former Intelligence Officer of the Tarnobrzeg District. I was, therefore, still quite well informed about everything that went on in the country and in the town. I did not know why, but I felt quite secure.

Our life was very quiet. We had a nanny goat that had awful rickets and ate everything. After a week or so she began to be choosy and Andrew, who used to take her to graze, had difficulty in keeping her where he wanted her. We milled our own flour by hand from the wheat from the College and Irena baked her own bread. The goat was milked twice a day and we had about two pints of milk daily. The coffee, made of roasted wheat, was very good with the goat's milk. Although the Vistula, running about a hundred yards behind the house, was very much depleted, I was able to supplement our diet with an occasional fish, which with milk, bread and the pig back-fat left over from my business dealings, kept us all in quite good trim.

One day, coming home from the College, I saw four NKVD men in front of the house chatting to the landlady. Irena was at the window, listening. I could do nothing but join the company. The landlady said, 'Here comes the teacher.' The NKVD sergeant, whom I knew to be the real boss of the NKVD outfit, was suitably impressed. In Russia the profession of teacher bears the stamp of political respectability. Nevertheless the sergeant started to ask me questions: where was I from, what was I teaching, who were my parents, and so on. I answered the man in accordance with my official papers and he seemed quite satisfied. Then he went over to Irena and started talking to her. She answered him in broken Russian. After a few minutes the sergeant said, 'You must be an educated woman.' I had to admire the man. It was only the second time during the war that either I or my wife had been taken for educated people.

The first time it had happened was in 1939. After my release from the Russian prison, a release engineered by Irena, we had all the official travel documents and were travelling by horse and cart (stolen) along the right bank of the River Bug. At dusk, armed with the official documents, we asked the Chairman of the Revolutionary Committee of the village we came to for shelter for the night. We were put up in the kitchen of the Chairman's home. At around 9 pm people started flocking into the room and I was soon engaged in a vivid discussion about the war, politics and so on. I was driving horses, I was dirty and unshaven, I was wearing an old Jewish overcoat I had found on the road and I was speaking Ukrainian, as did all the other men in the room. The room was lit with a small paraffin lamp and thick with coarse tobacco smoke. When, around midnight, the men started to leave, the Chairman said to me, 'You must either be an officer or a civil servant.'

I did not grasp the meaning of such a statement at the time. But now, when the NKVD sergeant said the same thing to a woman, clad in a cheap, mended blouse, speaking broken Russian, I suddenly understood. When talking to these people it did not matter what you said. It was not how the thoughts or statements were spoken. It was how they were formulated and how they were put over. The NKVD man was an educated man (as they all were), taught how to recognize, from a simple discussion, the background of the person he was talking to. That was why it was so difficult for an educated person to fool them.

161

The end of July, 1945, came. The College term had another three weeks to go. One day, when the town was again full of Russian troops going home, I went fishing. At the river I met about a hundred Russian soldiers who had just finished bathing. A group of them were listening to a young man sitting naked on the stump of a tree. Near him, on the grass, there lay the uniform of a Captain. They all belonged to the 117th Stalin's Armoured Guards Brigade, which I had encountered nearly a year before. Fortunately I could not recognize any of them. The Captain was talking about his exploits in Germany. The immense penis between his thighs had tell-tale syphilitic boils on it.

'I am glad I am going home,' he was saying. 'I have had enough of f. . . .g and f. . . .g and f. . . .g all the time. I have f. . . .d old women and young but what I liked most was f. . . .g small girls in front of their mothers, when the girls were crying "*Mutti, Mutti*". I f. . . .d them and often they died under me. But I have had enough. I had gonorrhea but I did not bother about it. But now I have syphilis, I have had enough of f. . . .g and I am glad to go home at last.'

The Captain reminded me of the Commandant of Sandomierz, a General who told a delegation of citizens complaining about the rape of a small girl, 'I do not understand your complaint. The c. .t is for f. . . .g, is it not?'

I listened to the captain, the hair on my neck tingling, and I felt sick. There was something inhuman in that boasting. The Germans were bad enough. The tortures, the inhuman treatment of the inmates of the concentration camps, the mass gassing of the Jews and other ethnic minorities, the genocide perpetrated by the SS and the Gestapo—all was known to me. With all this the Germans were just degenerate Europeans. But that Captain seemed inhuman, someone from a different planet. I was glad to see them going back to town.

Time and time again during my fishing expeditions, when sitting quietly, waiting hopefully for the float to move, I was stopped by young men, single or in small groups, all armed,

162

with grim determination on their faces. They were from the former 2nd Division of the Home Army and knew me quite well. They were roaming the countryside, not knowing quite what to do. They were, however, well informed about what was going on. From them I learned that Tench, Grey and others had been arrested and that in July, the other Grey had sprung them all from the Kielce jail; that Tench did not want to go but Grey made him. Tench died the same day of a heart attack. Many of the men from my old command had also been arrested, some put to death. The news which affected me most was that all men in the Opatow and neighbouring districts bearing the name of Szymanski, the official name I had had under the Germans, were being arrested and that the former C.O. of the Opatow District had been sentenced to death *in absentia*. As the days went on, I realized that arrests of my namesakes were increasing all the time and approaching Tarnobrzeg.

I am sure that the reason I still survived was that on the one hand the NKVD had been busy further west and on the other that Tarnobrzeg was a railway terminal. The town was teeming with thousands of civilians coming and going in all directions and every night train after train discharged troops, tanks and ammunition at the station. I ventured to go down there one afternoon. Tanks were all around it. Nearly every tank was daubed with '*Nach Berlin*' or '*Nach London*' (To Berlin, to London). I wondered what the political commissars could say to the troops to justify London as the final goal. In the dirt of the road I saw spread-eagled the flattened corpse of a Soviet soldier. In the words of an NKVD major on another occasion: 'It does not matter. We have many of them.'

I was appalled by the waste of grain, stored in huge heaps along the railway tracks. Funnily enough, as a method of storage, it proved to be cheap and successful. A few days of rain and the upper layers of the grain formed an impermeable crust, protecting the rest.

163

The Underground was working again, distributing all kinds of illegal literature. In every one General Anders, C.O. of the 2nd Polish Corps in Italy, appealed to the members of the Home Army to escape and to join him in Italy.

Nevertheless I knew that my time was up.

XVI

The Two Towers

Together we will take the road that leads
   into the West,
And far away will find a land where both our
   hearts may rest.

                Tolkien. *The Two Towers*

IN AUGUST, DURING the last of my lessons at the College, I was rounding off my talk about the structure of matter. I mentioned the energy-matter relationship and that in theory, if a chain reaction could be set up in, say, uranium, a bomb could be obtained with a fantastic destructive power.

Normally my talks caused no special reaction. This day, however, my pupils started to ask more and more questions about the problems of this chain reaction, the energy released by such a bomb, etc. I answered these questions to the best of my knowledge and eventually asked the class why this sudden interest. One of the class answered, 'Sir, yesterday, according to the BBC, the Americans dropped an atom bomb on Hiroshima.'

I froze. 'Well,' I said 'this is the end of an era and sooner or later it will be the end of our civilization.'

I went home. After a long talk with Irena we decided to get out of the country. Irena would sell everything we had (some of our belongings had been dug up from hiding places at Irena's sister's villa near Warsaw) and convert all the money

165

thus obtained into dollars. I would have to go to Cracow to arrange our escape. There was little time. Irena was pregnant. She had very nearly had a miscarriage after falling off a bicycle. She was expecting the child in February, 1946.

And so off I went, with one foot on the back of a lorry. I reached Cracow after two days and made straight for the new address of my uncle, a grand old man and the head of the family. He was a mining engineer by profession, and had made a fortune in Siberia at the end of the last century digging for emeralds. He then switched over to coal mining, first in the Don district of Russia and after the First World War in Poland, where he became involved in coal mining and banking. He nearly went bankrupt in the crash of the Bank for Commerce in Warsaw: he was one of the directors and when the affairs of the Bank were beginning to go wrong, he refused to sell his shares as all other directors did. During the war his flat was taken over by the Gestapo who had their headquarters nearby. Having practically nothing left of his fortune, he managed to acquire another one by dealing in antiques of all things! Again he lost everything in the Warsaw uprising and when he opened the door of his flat in Cracow to me he was wearing an old jacket and evening dress trousers. He met me as if nothing had happened to either of us. I trusted him explicitly, explained to him the situation and straight away the old gentleman offered me his help.

'First of all, my boy,' he said, 'you need some rest.'

We had some bread and dripping for our supper and I went happily to sleep on a spare sofa in the room. In the morning my uncle proudly brought me my breakfast in bed: toasted black bread and porridge cooked the Scottish way. He was very happy and proud to be able to serve me.

The same morning I met the rest of my family and in town I met Dahlia of all people. Dahlia was arranging her own exit from the country. She already knew all the ropes and through her I was able to obtain from the Czechoslovakian consul an entry visa into Czechoslovakia. The visa, or rather a special pass, was issued to me and to my family to go west in search of members of my family deported by the Germans during the war. The cost: fifty dollars, half of all that I had.

We also discussed the problem of which way to go. Dahlia was of the opinion that I should go the same way all people leaving the country were going: to Katowice in Upper Silesia and from there by train to Prague, going through the border station of Bohumin. According to the grapevine, there were no problems in entering Czechoslovakia at Bohumin, provided one had the necessary entry document. I could not make up my mind at this stage. I went back to Irena.

When I reached Tarnobrzeg she had already sold all our things. We had a further fifty dollars and some zlotys left over.

On 20 September, 1945, we left Tarnobrzeg surreptitiously. We had a small suitcase, a rucksack and, taped to Andrew's tummy, all our true, salvaged documents: Irena's Naval Identity Card and mine, Irena's diploma from the Warsaw Technical University, Andrew's birth certificate and our pre-war passports. Irena could not resist packing into the rucksack the album of family photographs and, of all things, her last pre-war ballgown, made of about twenty yards of pure silk.

Off we went. The first day we managed to reach Bochnia, about thirty miles east of Cracow, where we rested for the night with the elder of Irena's sisters. The next day we were in Cracow itself, staying with the family. We managed to buy on the black market some Czech kronen and a few thousand German Occupation marks in 1000-mark notes. On the 25th, after an emotional farewell, we were sitting in an open lorry going to Katowice. We decided not to go through Bohumin, but through Cieszyn, further south, a border town with Czechoslovakia.

The lorry driver had already started the engine when a commotion arose at the back of the lorry. A Captain in Polish uniform but with NKVD flashes, had thrown an elderly woman off the lorry and against all protests had taken a seat on

167

the bench near me. Only then had he ordered the driver to start.

The journey lasted for about four hours. It seemed an eternity to me because all this time the NKVD Captain was looking at me pensively. Our destination was the main square at Katowice. The Captain, however, stopped the lorry on the outskirts and disappeared. I did not like this at all. I therefore stopped the lorry when it had reached the main Katowice railway station. The lorry went off and I took my family on to the steps leading to a Red Army canteen. The steps were hidden from the station and from the street by a thick privet hedge. We sat down on the steps to eat some bread and waited, Russian soldiers going up and down the steps near us all the time.

After about fifteen minutes several cars and lorries full of soldiers burst into the station square. In a few minutes the station was cordoned off and a thorough search of all people at the station had begun. The search lasted for about half an hour. I felt sure that they were looking for me and my family. The Captain must have recognized me (after all, so many people knew me by sight). After leaving the lorry he must have alerted the Security people and, not finding me at the main square, they must have checked with the lorry driver and had been told that I left the lorry at the station. They left the station empty-handed.

Many years later I was told that the NKVD and the security people were two days behind me all the time from the moment we left Tarnobrzeg, and that the moving spirit behind the search was the old lawyer Polikier, who could not forget that his son had had to leave the estate on which he had been hiding.

At about 2 pm Irena and Andrew and I took the first train leaving Katowice. It did not matter where it was going; we had to leave the town. It went to Bielsko, a town about fifty kilometres from Cieszyn. There were no trains from Bielsko to Cieszyn, but we managed to scrounge a lift on a Russian lorry and at about 8.45 pm we reached Cieszyn. Tired but happy, we walked to the bridge and the border control post. We showed our pass but, alas, we were too late. We were told to wait until the next morning. The border post closed at 9 pm. It was nine-thirty.

With heavy hearts we started walking back to town. We had no idea what would happen to us then. We had virtually no Polish money left and every hotel required an identification document. But God was aware of our plight. On our way back to town we met Mr Smotrycki in the street, a man with whom I had spent a few weeks in 1942 at the 'safe' house at Planta belonging to Mr and Mrs Morawski. We greeted each other effusively and then Mr Smotrycki asked us what we were doing in this God-forsaken town. I explained. We were going to Czechoslovakia to look for our relatives. The border post was unfortunately closed.

Mr Smotrycki looked at me, smiled and said,

'No problem. I am, for the time being at least, the Mayor of this town and I will get you through quite easily.'

We went back to the border post. After a few words with the officer in charge (a Pole) the barrier went up. We thanked Mr Smotrycki and blessed him. We said goodbye. The officer saluted us and said, 'Good luck to all of you.' We crossed the bridge and were in Czechoslovakia.

Cieszyn was a small sleepy town. The border guards found our passes quite in order and even gave us the address of an hotel, cheap but respectable. Having registered at the hotel we were issued with some food coupons, ate a frugal meal and, having thanked God in our prayers, we went to sleep, dog-tired but with hope in our hearts for the future.

The next morning we boarded the express train from Kosice to Prague without any difficulties. Our papers were not checked. The first stop was Bohumin. But the train was stopped immediately, and surrounded by military and police; all the doors were closed and nobody was allowed onto the platform. We began to feel rather apprehensive. But nothing

169

happened to the passengers on our train. We were just waiting. After about fifteen minutes a train from Poland, packed with people, rolled slowly into the next but one platform. Immediately the train was surrounded by the police and the security forces and all the passengers were taken under escort to the station building. With a sigh of relief I had to thank God again. If we had taken the direct route to Prague we would have been on that train and our fate would have been sealed.

Soon afterwards our train began to move again. Andrew was in and out of the compartment all the time, enjoying the novelty of travelling in a coach with a corridor, tidy and comfortable. Very soon he came to us with a middle-aged Czech couple. The couple were quite impressed by Andrew's behaviour. They introduced themselves as Mr and Mrs Joseph Bunda from Prague, returning home from an expedition to obtain some food, which was scarce there. In the ensuing conversation (in broken Polish and Czechoslovakian) it transpired that the couple were of the Hussite faith and when they learned that my family and I were Protestants, they invited us to stay with them in Prague. If we agreed, our life would be much easier. All the hotels were full, everyone had to have a permit to stay, etc. With grateful thanks we accepted their kind offer.

The Bundas lived with their daughter near Hradcany Castle in the old part of the town. They had one bedroom and a large kitchen. Against our protests, we were put into the bedroom, which had one huge bed in which all three of us could easily sleep in comfort. The Bundas and their daughter arranged to sleep in the kitchen.

'Tonight we eat,' said Mr Bunda. 'Then we all have a good rest and tomorrow we shall go to register you with the police.'

These last few words did not go down too well with us but we could do nothing about it and that was that. We ate with appetite the knedle, the Czechoslovakian national dish, which consists of pastry stuffed with plums, and after a common prayer we all went to bed.

In the morning, after a frugal breakfast, Mr Bunda seemed to be in no hurry to go to the police.

'No hurry, no hurry, the police will be at the station all morning,' he said.

We left for the police station at about 12.30. The police were very helpful. They registered me and my family, issued the required registration form and asked how long we intended to stay in Prague. I said about three weeks. At once a set of ration cards were issued, valid for three weeks, and after that the fateful sentence:

'Now the next step is for you to go to the Town Hall and register yourself and your family with the Security Police.' Saying this, the policeman looked at the clock and said, 'You cannot go to the Security Police today. It is Saturday and their office is already closed. You will have to wait until Monday morning. They open at 9 am.'

Not likely, thought I. As I thanked the police profusely, I understood why Mr Bunda had not been in a hurry to go to the police. An astute man, he knew what would be involved.

Going back home, we saw the Victory procession, with Field-Marshal Montgomery at its head, progressing slowly among the enthusiastic crowds towards Hradcany Castle. Not a single Russian soldier was in sight, only thousands and thousands of Czechs, delirious with joy. 'God Save the King' could be heard fortissimo. The Field-Marshal drove slowly past, only a few feet from us. I looked at him with mixed feelings of envy and admiration. With envy, not because of the Field-Marshal's military achievements, but because he was a free man and could return home. 'Home' was something we did not have any more.

Back at Mr Bunda's I asked him whether he and his country would not prefer to be under Western occupation instead of Russian. Mr Bunda answered this question very concisely:

'Throughout our history, up to 1939, we were Western orientated. Our culture, our civilization are Western. 1939 showed that the West had no interest in us or in our fate. We

171

had to turn to Russia to survive, and only the future will show whether we were right or wrong.'

That day Mrs Bunda spent all the three weeks' rations in one go. We all had a wonderful meal, after which I went to the address given to me in Cracow. For the last few months General Anders, the General commanding the 2nd Polish Corps in Italy, had been urging all Home Army personnel to leave Poland and to join him. The address in Prague was the link in the chain between Italy and Poland. There I obtained from a young man an official-looking travel permit to go to Pilsen, in the American-occupied zone. I could not understand, however, why it was that I had to pay fifty dollars for the document. They were the last American dollars we had left and somehow it did not seem right to me. Nevertheless, I paid and went back to Irena and Andrew. In the evening we all went to a circus, with Andrew brimming with excitement and as happy as he had never been before.

At 7 am on Sunday we were already at the main station. No permits needed to be shown to get tickets to Pilsen. At 0715 Irena, Andrew and I were on our way to the West.

There was a document check at the border between the two occupation zones. Again our consular paper proved to be sufficient. The Russians did not even bother to look at the Prague travel permit. Fifty dollars down the drain!

We were at Pilsen by about 10 am. From the station we made our way to the American Displaced Persons camp. Waiting to see the Commandant we suddenly saw Dahlia. Elegant and smiling, she had come to get her papers to enable her and her children to go and join her husband with the 2nd Polish Corps in Italy. She had come by train a few days earlier, via Bohumin, with plenty of money and all the luggage she wanted. Yes, money was a great help at such times!

Eventually, at about 2 pm, I was summoned into the presence of the U.S. Camp Commandant, a Major.

The interview was a short one and left me in a state of shock. Apparently the directives of General Eisenhower were quite

172

explicit. No civilians from Poland or Czechoslovakia were allowed into the American Occupation Zone of Germany. He had to obey orders and therefore had to refuse permission for me and my family to enter the camp. Full stop. Out!

I broke down completely. Six years of fighting, of eluding Germans officially and Russians unofficially, the last seven months hiding, running, outwitting the best and the most ruthless of all intelligence networks, with only God guiding my every step and inspiring every move; at last reaching people whom I considered to be our friends and protectors; only to be turned away, back to the world I was trying to leave behind me. To go back and live only for a few weeks more.

I was shaking like a leaf, unable to control myself any more, as I had been doing successfully for all these years!

And then Irena stepped in. In no uncertain terms she told me off. She told me not to be a sissy, to pick myself up and to be a man again, not to behave like a woman on the verge of hysteria. She took me by one hand and Andrew by the other. She told us to pick up our belongings and led us out of the camp and to the station. At the station she was told that, in order to obtain a ticket to the border station, we must first obtain a pass from the Town Hall. She took us to the Town Hall, found the man authorized to issue the necessary permits, persuaded the man to issue one for us, then took us back to the station. She bought the tickets and at about 4 pm we were off by train, destination West.

By that time I was calm again. During the journey we had our papers inspected by the Border Gendarmerie, with an elderly gendarme in charge. He came to us later on, explaining that it would be no use for us to alight at Furst-im-Wald, the border station in Germany. We would be turned back by the Americans. He was very sympathetic and suggested that, instead of going West directly by train, we go with him to the border post a few miles away. He offered us a place to stay at the border post and told us that the next morning, after we had

173

had a rest and something to eat, he would show us how and where to cross the border with Germany, avoiding the American patrols. This way we could have a chance. Otherwise we would have none.

We accepted the offer with gratitude. The Border Gendarmerie seemed to be without any security people in that locality, the gendarmes seemed to be decent chaps, and anyway we had no choice.

We alighted at a deserted stop and were warmly greeted by the personnel of the border post. We were given a meal and then went to sleep in a separate room with three beds and plenty of blankets to keep us warm in the chill of the autumn night.

We woke at 6 am. The sky was overcast, it was cold and raining really hard. We had breakfast with the others: substitute coffee, bread and sausage. The cook even prepared a pack of sandwiches for our journey. After breakfast everyone present took part in the discussion about the direction we should take in order to cross the border. A detailed map of the region was produced and, since I had no compass, all the salient points on our way were pointed out and described. We would have to cross the railway-line running through the valley and then three mountain ridges separated by two other valleys, fortunately without rivers. We should be all right once we had crossed the two valleys and the three mountain ridges.

After thanking the hospitable Czechs and making a short prayer, we went off into the countryside and into the sheets of rain blocking the distant view of the mountains. Irena and I carried a small suitcase each. Andrew had a small haversack and all the original documents still strapped to his tummy.

The going was very heavy and we were all soon soaked to the skin. All the time we had to scramble up, then down, through brush, bracken, fern. Irena and I soon became tired; only Andrew kept going strongly (a short spell in the Boy

Scouts at Tarnobrzeg had helped him), whistling and singing, helping us both and keeping our morale high, so that we could go on scrambling, falling, rising again and keeping on. He was seven years old.

At about 6 pm, utterly exhausted, we emerged from the forest on the last ridge on to a large, cultivated field with a barn in the middle. The barn seemed to be of a different style from the ones we had seen during the day. We decided that we were by now in occupied territory. We ate some of our sandwiches, drank some rain water, buried ourselves deep in hay and were soon unconscious to the world around us, deep in sleep.

XVII

The Friendly West?

WE WERE AWAKENED at about 6 am by prodding and shouting. The barn was full of Germans. They seemed to be uncertain of themselves, even afraid, and were armed with forks, spades and truncheons. Excitedly they asked me to get up and told me that they would have to take us to the Americans. I sighed with relief. We were in Germany and, after all, to contact the Americans in Germany was the object of the exercise.

During the long rest our clothes had dried, the rain had stopped and although we were hungry, we went contentedly with the Germans to the nearest American post. It was not far off. We had slept about a mile from the border and soon a solitary American sergeant stepped out of a small hut at the roadside and confronted us with a coldly-set face. He listened to the explanations given in broken English by the leader of the German party and then turned to me.

'Nothing doing,' he said. 'My orders are to turn back all people crossing the border from Czechoslovakia. I won't listen to any arguments. You just sit yourselves down. A lorry will come and take you all back to Pilsen.'

That was that. I was dumb with despair again but by now I had become used to disappointments. My mind went completely blank. I did not and could not think clearly any more. Irena and Andrew were also quiet. We all sat down on a fallen tree, ate the rest of our sandwiches and without a word waited for our fate to come.

Meanwhile the guard was changed at the border. The first sergeant disappeared and another sergeant arrived for duty in a jeep. While the first sergeant was aloof and cold, the new one was more sympathetic. He started talking with us, asked many questions about the situation in Poland and Czechoslovakia. He wanted me to tell him why I and my family were trying to reach the West. I was quite frank with the sergeant. He listened attentively to the reasons I was giving him and then said,

'Listen, I have never seen you. I have never spoken to you. I don't know anything about you. Just take your family and leave me and the post. O.K.?'

I was speechless. I did not know what to say, how to thank this man. I wanted to express my gratitude in some way. We had one ring left, with a decent diamond. We offered it to the sergeant. He refused to take it, saying, 'Just leave, and God bless you.'

We turned our backs to the border and started walking along the empty road leading to the West.

There was a beer cellar a few hundred yards down the road. We were all thirsty. We went in to buy some beer and a drink for Andrew. The place was empty. We had our drinks and left. A few minutes later an American army lorry coming from the direction of Furst-am-Wald suddenly made a U-turn and screeched to a halt near us. Another sergeant ordered us to climb in, saying that the Counter-Intelligence Corps Captain wanted to see us.

Very soon we were at Furst-am-Wald and had stopped in front of the most imposing building in the town. We were led to a room on the first floor. The house was swarming with Germans, men and women, either waiting or talking to the American officers or NCOs behind the desks which occupied nearly every available space in the house. The crowd had a familiar look: all were agents or informers.

Irena, Andrew and I were eventually ushered into a room where an American Major was sitting behind a huge desk

177

strewn with papers. Without any preamble the Major started telling me off in a loud voice. What did we think we were doing? We had had orders to go back and we had disobeyed those orders. Those orders were, and still are, quite clear: all people coming from the east must go back to wherever they had come from. The Major started to shout louder and louder, as if he wanted everybody to hear him: these orders were to be obeyed, he would not tolerate . . . and so on and so on.

Andrew started to cry and, to my amazement, I saw that the Major was looking at Andrew, smiling and winking reassuringly. I could not understand what was going on and why the Major was behaving in this funny way. Eventually, after a long harangue, the Major sternly told us to leave the room and to wait at the entrance of the building for a jeep which would take us to the market place, where a lorry would come in due course and take us back to Pilsen. Another disappointment, another failure in our efforts to reach the West.

The driver of the jeep indeed took us to the market square, deposited us in front of the PX shop and drove off, without saying a single word. We waited on the pavement, looking at the square full of personnel carriers, armoured vehicles and soldiers. We did not want to look at the window display of the PX shop, full of chocolate bars, cigarettes and sausages.

After about an hour a civilian approached us, casually sauntering along the pavement. He stopped near us and, looking into the PX shop window, said to us in German, out of the corner of his mouth, 'The Major told you to go. Why are you still here?'

Only then did everything click into place in my mind. It was the same situation with which I had had to deal during the German occupation, when I was obliged to come to terms with two different ideas. Now it was the Americans who had to resolve the problem of conflicting ideas. On the one hand they had the official orders, dictated by political considerations (it did not matter whether the political considerations were right or wrong). On the other hand much was known

178

about the behaviour of the Russians and hence there was a will to help people whenever possible. The Major had to shout loudly about his carrying out the orders of the Allied High Command for everyone in his building to know about it. At the same time he had left a gate open for me and my family, so that we could escape without his official knowledge or approval.

We again took our belongings from the pavement and started walking towards the station.

Telling people that Guardian Angels exist and that they are sent to earth to help people is usually met with derision and laughter. I had, however, had the experience of meeting them.

I could still vividly remember the day in September, 1939, when we were going in our cart along the eastern bank of the River Bug, the demarcation line between the German- and Russian-occupied zones of Poland, trying to cross over to the German side. We were approaching the town of Brest Litovsk and the fort guarding the bridge over the river. The fort was on a small hill by the river bank, its slopes strewn with branches and trunks of trees mown down by bullets. To our right stretched an empty, recently-ploughed field. Beyond it, in the distance, we could see the suburbs of Brest Litovsk. The scene was one of utter desolation and emptiness. I was talking to Irena when, suddenly, just a few paces away we saw a small farm cart, drawn by a shaggy horse, with a solitary man driving it.

The man greeted us in the old manner: 'Let Jesus Christ be blessed.'

We told him that we would like to cross the river and he said,

'If you want to cross the river through the bridge inside the fort, you would have to go first to the NKVD in town to get a special permit. Personally speaking, I would not recommend you to do so. But,' he smiled, 'a kilometre downstream from here there is a pontoon bridge and there is no one guarding it. Why don't you cross the river there?'

179

I turned with relief to Irena to see her reaction to our good luck. When I turned back there was no man, no horse, no cart. The same emptiness as before. We did not hesitate. Off we went, and indeed, half a mile downstream, we saw a brand-new, unused, pontoon bridge. There was not a soul in sight. We crossed the bridge and that was that. We did not dare to look behind to see whether it was still there or not.

Something happened now on our way to the station which again reminded me of our crossing of the Bug and of the help we had had from a man who appeared from nowhere and disappeared into nowhere.

A man approached us in a side street. After greeting us he introduced himself as John, a Ukrainian, and said that he would like to help me and my family in any way he could. He had all the necessary papers to enable him to move around and all the necessary contacts in the town.

He asked what money we had and in what denominations. I answered that all the occupation money we had was in 1000-mark bank-notes. John said that these bank-notes were useless. The Russians were flooding the country with 1000-mark notes, far in excess of all agreements with the Allies, and by now the Western Powers had decided that the largest bank-notes valid for circulation were the 100-mark ones. However, he, John, had contacts, and for ten per cent for him, he could change the ten 1000-mark notes into smaller denominations. Would I trust him?

It seemed a foolish thing to do, but, without thinking about it and without realizing what I was doing, I handed all our money to John. We agreed to wait for him at the same place and he disappeared.

It suddenly dawned on us that we were fools. We did not know a thing about him. How could we have behaved like such simpletons? Despair started to creep into our minds again. But then—John was back, with a sheaf of 100-mark notes in one hand and a freshly-baked loaf of bread in the other! We were overwhelmed with joy and gratitude. We all started discussing what to do next. Again John made the decisions. He told us that, since he had the necessary permits, he would buy the tickets to Cham, the next town where there was a D.P. camp. He told us to go to the station and wait there for the train, which would leave for Cham the next morning at 6 am. John also said that the German police would try to prevent us boarding the train. He would therefore be waiting for us in the last carriage, which would be a luggage van. He would close the doors opening on to the platform. We would have to make our way to the other side of the train and, as soon as the police ended the search of the train for illegal passengers, he would slide open the door and we would have to jump in as the train was moving.

We went to the station, which was packed to capacity. Platforms, waiting rooms, even the square in front of the station building, were full of men, women and children, all waiting for the next train going east. A large contingent of German police were keeping this multitude in some sort of order. The stench was appalling. Some people seemed to be happy, some in despair. All were dirty, dishevelled. Lice could be seen crawling on the hair and clothing of nearly everyone.

It was now about 8 pm. I put Irena and Andrew in a corner of a waiting room, as far from the crowd as possible. Mother and son huddled together for warmth and tried to sleep. I could not. I started wandering around the station, trying to tire out the two German policemen who were following me all the time. I began to feel a cold determination and a sense of purpose coming to me.

You did not manage to catch me for five years or more, I thought. You will fail this time as well.

Seeing that I was doing nothing in particular, both policemen gradually began to lose interest in me. The night hours dragged on interminably.

I began to sway on my feet. I had been up since dawn, hope alternating with despair. I was thirsty and hungry and sleepy. All the same, I did not feel alone. The crowd was all around me

181

and, what was more important, my wife, with another life inside her, and my son were sleeping peacefully. It seemed as if they had handed over to me all their troubles and their hope, and were waiting peacefully among this miserable crowd for me to make all the decisions and to lead them to safety. I began to pray, and suddenly began to feel calm and at peace.

At about 5.30 am John appeared. Passing by, he whispered, 'Remember, the train is coming to the platform at six. Be behind the last coach, the luggage van.'

I went to wake up Irena and Andrew and told them to make for the end of the platform in an unhurried and casual manner. I myself went on to the platform in full view of the policemen who kept watch on the crowd, preventing anyone from approaching too near the track.

The train came in. Behind the crowd, which was trying to take it by force, with the police busy repelling them, Irena and Andrew and I jumped from the platform behind the luggage van and went to the other side of the train. The sliding doors of the van slid slightly open. It was John. He told us to wait until the inspection of the train was over. We waited. We heard John talking to the police, who then went through the rest of the train, throwing out all those who had boarded it without the necessary permits or documents. Then we heard the doors slamming and then the whistle. The train began to move. The door slid open again; Irena and I threw Andrew in, then in jumped Irena and eventually Irena, with John's help, managed to hoist me in. John said a hurried 'Good-bye' and jumped out, just managing to catch the end of the platform. We were under way. The train was completely empty. We left the luggage van and sat in the coach next to it. The weather was miserable, with overcast skies and a drizzle, leaving smudges on the dirty windows.

The train stopped after about half an hour. We looked out and saw the name Cham on a miserable shack by a single platform in an open field. We then left the train. There was no one around, no ticket collector, no guard. A total emptiness.

We started towards the town which we could see about a mile away. Entering the town we saw a gate with a huge notice: Cham Transient D.P. Camp. We went in. The commandant, a Yugoslav, greeted us warmly but said that it was not in his power to accept us without the authorization of the American military authorities. Seeing the state we were in, he said that there was no hurry. We would have to be deloused first, then eat and sleep, and the next day I would be taken to the Americans. We were sprinkled liberally with DDT, were issued with six tins of sardines and a loaf of bread. We ate and went to sleep between clean blankets. At midday we again had sardines and went to sleep until the evening. We repeated the performance in the evening and were again in bed by about 9 pm.

The next morning I took all our documents from Andrew's tummy and was taken in a lorry to Cham to see the American in charge. Apparently the Americans knew already that I was coming. I was greeted in Polish by a well-dressed individual who said that he was a Rumanian oil man, temporarily acting as an interpreter for the Americans. He knew several languages, including, of course, English. Together we went to the first floor, to a door bearing the name Captain C. Hanson, C.I.C. When opening the door the Rumanian said in English, 'Captain, this is the father of the Polish family escaping to the West, about which you were notified yesterday.' The Rumanian did not know that I spoke English!

I began to have mixed feelings. I was apprehensive about the outcome of this meeting with the American. At the same time I was really touched. Rejecting me and my family officially, unofficially the Americans had been keeping tabs on us all the time! There was the civilian who had told us to go away; there was John, feeding us and helping us all the way. I realized again that the Americans, like everyone else, had official and unofficial standards: standards reflecting the official policy and standards reflecting the true feelings and attitude of the Army personnel, bless them!

183

I greeted Captain Hanson in my rusty English, gave him my rank and displayed in front of him all my original documents: my Naval Identity Card, damaged but still legible, Irena's Naval Identity Card and her Diploma Certificate from the Warsaw Technical University stating her academic title, Eng. Dip., and lastly Andrew's birth certificate. Captain Hanson looked through all the papers for a long time and then asked me briefly to tell him our story.

I did not hesitate to tell him the truth. I told how I had been arrested by the Germans on 11 November, 1939; how in February, 1940, I had escaped and had been down the escape route to join the Polish Navy in Great Britain. Following the first mass arrests in Kielce, the first stage of my escape route, I had received orders to stay in Poland and join the official Underground. I told the Captain that in May, 1941, I had been appointed C.O. of the Opatow District of the Home Army, that my name was included in the first issue of the *Fahnungs Blatt*; that in order to protect my men I had had to retaliate against the communists under Russian command; that I was under sentence of death by the communists and the Russians; that all my colleagues who had had the misfortune to fall into the hands of communists had been brutally murdered; that arrests of the members of the Home Army and arrests of political leaders other than communists were going on all the time; that for nine months I had managed, with God's help, to elude the NKVD and the Secret Police, but eventually, knowing the thoroughness of the NKVD's methods I realized that I had no chance of surviving and that, moreover, I could see no purpose in fighting on and had decided therefore to seek refuge in the West.

I told the Captain that we had been turned away by the Commandant of the D.P. camp in Pilsen. I did not dwell on the means by which we had managed to reach Cham.

'That is all, Captain. Here we are and here we hope to stay,' I said at last.

The Captain had listened very attentively. Then he started

184

to ask detailed questions about the political and economic situation in Poland. I answered him to the best of my knowledge and as objectively as I possibly could. Eventually Captain Hanson said,

'I see that they are trying to exterminate the intelligentsia.'

'Yes,' I agreed.

Captain Hanson stamped a sheet of paper and handed it over to me saying that he hereby authorized the Camp Commandant in Cham to admit us into the camp and provisionally to register me and my family as Displaced Persons. I thanked the Captain profusely and was taken back to the camp. We were at home. Or so I thought.

XVIII

In the American Zone

FIVE DAYS AFTER my visit to the C.I.C. we were taken by a lorry to Regensburg, where we were registered as fully-fledged D.P.s. All the time we were fed on Portuguese sardines, morning and evening—*toujours des sardines*. After a while I could not stand them any more. True, there was also bread, margarine and boiled mutton, and all free, so we did not complain too much.

In Regensburg I went to the Red Cross to try to locate my parents and a week later we had their address. They were in Palestine and a month afterwards we had a letter from them.

My mother was delirious with joy. They knew from the man who had left Poland in my place in 1940 that I had joined the Underground. When the war in Europe ended, none of my parents' friends and acquaintances could understand why they did not try to find me. Their answer was proof of our mutual understanding and our knowledge of the situation: if he is alive, it is up to him to look for us, and he will do it when it is safe for him to do so. If we start looking for him, we might put his life in jeopardy. They were right.

From Regensburg we were all transferred to the officers' PoW camp in Upper Bavaria, south of Munich. We were glad to go. For the members of the Home Army Murnau was one of the stages on the way to Italy and the Polish 2nd Corps.

At Murnau we were initially billeted separately, Irena and Andrew in the women's quarters, myself in the main officers'

186

block. I threw myself heart and soul into the social life of the camp. I became an active member of the Home Army Association. I tried, without much success, to lecture on the situation in Poland and on possible methods of guerrilla warfare. I played chess, bridge and poker.

Irena tried to have some fillings done and to crown a few of her teeth which had been badly neglected during the war. After many enquiries she found a highly recommended dentist in the town. Having had her teeth prepared for crowning and filling she went to see him and found that he had been arrested. He was a member of the Gestapo.

After a few weeks we were given a small detached bungalow on the former SS estate in the town itself. There were two bedrooms, a living room and all amenities. And after we had settled down in our new home we met George.

George was about twenty-one, a member of the Home Army who had had rather a chequered career. His father, a member of the Polish Socialist Party, had been hanged by the Germans in 1940. George was then sixteen. He joined the Home Army in a commuter suburb near Warsaw and at the ripe age of seventeen became a member of the execution squad, in which he was very active. In 1942 he was arrested and sent by the Germans to work as a slave labourer at one of the factories in Düsseldorf. He was caught sabotaging some machinery, arrested, tortured and put into solitary confinement—actually, not quite solitary, because the Germans put into his cage an Alsatian dog, trained to bite his ankles every time he tried to sit or lie down. Neither George nor the dog had much sleep for three days. As he was being taken to be interrogated again, he killed the one guard with him with his bare hands and escaped from the detention building. He already had contacts in town, so he went to see a man who supplied him with suitable false documents and the same night he was on a train to Poland. A timely air raid diverted the Germans from an attempt to recapture him.

After his return home he found himself 'blown' many times

over, so he went to the east and joined the Wolyn Division of the Home Army. After the Division had been disarmed by the Russians during STORM and all its officers shot, he became a member of a new group of partisans, fighting the Russians under the leadership of a certain Oliwa (Oil). In 1945 the group moved nearer Warsaw and began to operate there, with the self-imposed task of protecting Polish women against rape by the Russians. His own method, at any rate, was simple: having tracked down the perpetrator of the crime, he would cosh him, tie him to a tree, cut off his penis and leave him to bleed to death. Although the Russians did not care much about their losses they decided that this kind of thing had to be stopped. The resulting operations of the NKVD and of the Polish security forces compelled the group to disappear. They disappeared in style: twenty of them, armed to the teeth, went south and, after crossing half the country on foot, entered Czechoslovakia in Sudetenland in September, 1945. They wanted, of course, to join General Anders in Italy.

Their march through Poland deserves a separate book. George did not tell me all the details, but their experiences illustrated very clearly the Polish character: throughout their journey they could always find shelter. The Polish peasant is a wily character. All the Soviet propaganda left him unmoved. He looked on, and drew his own conclusions. I remembered an occasion back in 1944 when a Soviet Colonel in command of a regiment established his Command Post at a house in a village south of the Holy Cross Mountains. In order to show his respect for the Colonel a villager laid the table for lunch with an elegant tablecloth and the best of his tableware. When the Colonel and his Staff sat down to eat, the villager proudly put in the middle of the table a large dish piled high with crayfish. When he saw the Colonel brushing half the crayfish on to his own plate with his hand, he left the room disgusted, exclaiming, 'And they call themselves officers!'

George and his group were not so lucky in Czechoslovakia. The night after they crossed the border they were surrounded

188

by the security forces and the army. In the fierce engagement which followed all but George were either killed or taken prisoner. George survived because he managed to slip into a mountain stream and hide under a rock overhang. He stayed there for over twelve hours. When eventually the security forces withdrew he dried himself and went on his way. He did not like to talk about how he managed to cross Czechoslovakia or how he had come to register as a D.P.

He became part of our family. He called Irena 'Mama' and me 'Tata'. He was also very helpful in other ways: he was a fully-fledged black marketeer, buying from the Americans and selling on a large scale everything he could get hold of. The Americans used to sell on the black market such products as sugar, coffee, flour, tinned meat, sweets—anything they could get at the PX. They claimed that it did no harm because all the supplies were allocated with an excess of twenty-five per cent to cover losses. 'Waste' within this percentage was OK. Hell, however, broke loose if more than twenty-five per cent disappeared. I remember one evening at our house when George haggled with an American sergeant over the price of a lorry-load of sugar. The American wanted too much. George could not raise the amount required and so the American went to town to sell the sugar direct to the Germans.

George managed to buy an old German Army motorcycle. He got some petrol from the Americans but could not ride the bike himself. I could, and twice we went to a farm near Garmisch Partenkirchen to buy some beef, paying with cigarettes. It was fun to have George riding as a passenger, a huge rucksack on his shoulders, bursting at its seams with beef and dripping with blood. We had no driving licence, nor any kind of insurance, nor even a permit. Fortunately, Germans in 1946, including the police, were rather timid and subdued. Twice we were stopped by traffic police. They looked at the bike, at us, at the rucksack and both times waved us on without a word.

On 11 February, 1946 Irena was delivered of a girl at the

189

local German hospital, in a crude but effective manner. We called our daughter Eleonora Ewa. She was ash-blonde and beautiful.

I was told that there was a Polish Navy liaison officer at Regensburg. I managed to get a lift on a lorry going that way and tried to contact the officer, but I could not find him. Apparently he had already left. Disappointed, I took the same lorry back to Murnau. Just before Munich we met a road block: two light tanks, about a platoon of, infantry and two machine-guns covering the road. A young Lieutenant came to check the driver's travel warrant. Then he suddenly turned to me and told me that I was under arrest.

'Why?' I asked.

'Because you are wearing an American battle-dress uniform to which you have no right.'

'But,' I replied, 'it was issued to me by the American authorities.'

'I don't know about that. You are under arrest.'

He was very young, he was in command of a road block and he was probably hoping to catch some big SS fish. He had authority and he had to show it somehow.

I was furious, but said to myself, 'He wants me and he shall have me.' I took my belongings from the lorry and started walking towards one of his trucks.

'Where do you think you are going?' shouted the Lieutenant.

'I am under arrest, am I not? You have to take me with you.'

I saw panic in his eyes. He must have had second thoughts about his decision. After a while he said condescendingly,

'Well, I'll let you go this time. But watch it.'

'What should I watch?' I asked.

'Never you mind. Off you go.'

Two hours later I was back in Murnau.

I then tried to contact the Polish Navy Mission at SHAPE in Paris. The camp C.O. managed to obtain a travel warrant for me and one evening I caught the American forces' train to

190

Paris. We travelled all night. We slept and had a meal at the completely destroyed station at Stuttgart and stopped again at Metz. Never, even in my imagination, had I seen so much food in such variety. Europe was starving, yet on the train I saw half of what had been piled on my plate thrown away.

In Paris I was able to change some Occupation marks into French francs and found a small room in a shabby hotel in Montmartre which I could afford. It took me three days to make the necessary contacts but they could do nothing for me. The Polish authorities in London had had to agree under pressure from the British not to take any more Polish Navy officers back into the Navy, which was still under British command. The only way I could rejoin my Navy was to come to Britain as a civilian. I had no idea how to manage this.

During those three days, since I had very little money, I could not afford proper meals at any of the restaurants or even the bistros. The only food I could afford were oysters, which for some unknown reason were very cheap. I used to have a dozen for breakfast, for lunch and for the evening meal, with bread, which was given away free with them. I felt somewhat apprehensive when I started on this diet. I had read that oysters were an aphrodisiac, used by the Romans and in later times, for instance, by King Louis XII of France, who ate oysters and drank spiced wine in an effort to perpetuate his dynasty. Happily the oysters had no effect whatsoever. Sardine saturation probably acted as a buffer.

I returned to Murnau and, in March, 1946, I went, or rather was taken, to Italy. I went alone. At that time no children were allowed to come under the aegis of the Polish 2nd Corps.

XIX

In Italy

THE CORPS HEADQUARTERS was in Ancona at the time. I was taken to the reception centre at Porto San Giorgio, about thirty kilometres south of Ancona on the Adriatic coast. As I suspected, I was not allowed to join the Polish army. Through the intermediary of his adjutant, General Anders said that 'He never had needed, and will never need, any Naval personnel in his corps.'

I was thus stuck in Italy, with Irena and the children still in Germany, with no prospects, no money and little hope for the future.

I was fortunate, nevertheless, in that the Lutheran chaplain of the Corps, the Reverend W. Fierla, whose services I managed to attend, helping him by playing the organ, became my friend and one day he came to see me and, without any preamble, said, 'Your wife and children are in Italy, at the Red Cross centre at Verona.'

He offered me his jeep and driver and the next day I was reunited with my family, to find my daughter dying of gastroenteritis.

The story of Irena's crossing into Italy showed again the way in which God was working in our lives. There was no official way in which children could be taken to Italy. The officer in charge of Home Army female personnel in Marnau decided on a very simple expedient: simply to put Irena and the children on the lorry transporting those women officially

192

accepted by the 2nd Corps and hope for the best. The transport stopped at Innsbruck and a Polish officer appeared in his car to take charge. He started to read out the names. Then he suddenly stopped, went over to Irena and asked, 'Are you the daughter of Mrs Maria Sagajllo? I knew Mrs Sagajllo very well before the war when I was the director of a tyre factory and Mrs Sagajllo was Head of the Rubber Research Laboratory of the Ministry of Defence.'

When Irena told him that she was her daughter-in-law the man decided that would he would go as driver of his official car, Irena would go as his passenger, Andrew would travel in the boot, and Eleonora would lie on the back seat, carefully covered with blankets, and hopefully, asleep.

The arrangement worked perfectly. The M.P.s at the border did not even check the car of the officer in charge of the transport. The border at Brenner was passed and Irena and the children were safely deposited at the Red Cross centre at Verona where the man took his leave.

At the centre, since Irena could not feed her daughter herself any more, one of the nurses gave the child some evaporated milk. The milk was not sufficiently diluted, and Eleonora became severely ill with gastroenteritis. Irena had kept her alive by giving her water every few minutes, to avoid total dehydration.

The driver took us all back to Port San Giorgio. We managed to find a room in the town with two very nice women, Senora Principi and her daughter Maria. By this time my parents were sending me parcels, each containing about three thousand cigarettes. By selling them we had enough money to feed ourselves and to buy milk for the baby. The milk, skimmed and diluted, kept our daughter alive. It is a sad reflection on our people, but one out of every three parcels sent to us from Palestine used to disappear in the post.

In August, 1946, all civilian personnel, men, women and children, were transferred to a transit camp at Barletta, near Bari in Southern Italy. It was very hot, very dusty and for a change the meals consisted of boiled mutton and peas. Eleonora was barely alive, all skin and bones.

Every day parties of men and women who had relatives in Britain would leave the camp. We could not go. We had no relatives there. As usual, Providence lent a hand. A very distant cousin of mine, a Lieutenant in the 2nd Corps, had been posted to the camp as a member of its administration. It took us some time to find and to recognize each other, but when we did, he was able to provide us with an affidavit that I was a cousin of a member of the Polish 2nd Corps on active service, and that as such I had the right to enter Great Britain. I do not know what happened to him afterwards.

One day in September Andrew and I were taken to Naples where we boarded a transport ship bound for Glasgow. Since the ship had no amenities for small children, Irena and Eleonora were left behind at Barletta. We had a solemn promise from the Camp Commandant that she would be able to join me as soon as special transport for women and babies could be organized

Eleonora was so weak that, a few days after our departure, Irena had to take her to hospital. The staff was incompetent and, instead of improving, the child became worse, having caught a chest infection. Irena was furious. She had quite a row with the doctors, took her child away and started to look around for a good paediatrician. She was lucky and found one eventually, the paediatric professor at the University of Bari, who lived in Barletta. Since Irena had virtually no money the professor helped her to sell a diamond ring. That allowed her to pay the professor's fee and enabled him to buy on the black market injections of heavy doses of Vitamin D. The child started to improve from the day of the first injection. All the same, they both had to wait for another two and a half months before they could start on their own journey to Britain.

194

XX

Great Britain—a new life

IT TOOK ANDREW and me nearly a week to reach Glasgow. Although officially a civilian, I was allowed to use the officers' quarters on the ship and I could therefore spend most of my time playing bridge. I could play only for very small stakes and yet by the end of the voyage I had won over five pounds. It was quite a sum to me at that time.

From Glasgow we were taken to a camp in Hull, from which I telephoned the Polish Naval Headquarters in London about my arrival in Great Britain. Three days later I received a first-class railway warrant with orders to report to the Plymouth Command. On 26 September, 1946, I officially rejoined the Polish Navy under British command, with the rank of Lieutenant-Commander, Executive Branch. I was also given a hundred pounds to buy my uniform and the rest of my equipment.

Although I knew everybody and everybody knew me, I felt an outsider to some extent. The days of the Polish Navy were over. Those Polish ships which had survived the war were either handed over to the Warsaw Government or were laid up by the British. The future was uncertain for everyone. Ernest Bevin was pressurizing all Poles to return to 'free' Poland. Everyone was anxious, and increasingly concerned about his own future to the exclusion of others.

I was waiting for Irena. Although I went to London twice to try to speed up her arrival, October was over and there was no

195

sign of her. Eventually I decided to go over the heads of my superiors. I sent a telegram direct to Major Owen, the Barletta Camp Commandant, stating that I was an officer in the Polish Navy, under British command, and yet nothing was being done about bringing my wife and child to Britain.

A week later Irena landed at Dover. She had travelled in November, in freezing weather, on a train supposedly specially arranged for young mothers and babies. The train had no heating at all. Steam from drying nappies filled the compartment and by the time the train reached Dover, most of the babies had severe colds and a few of them had pneumonia.

I went to London to fetch them, brought them to Plymouth to a rented flat and then went to collect Andrew from Hull where I had left him. In September, 1947, our third child, Patricia Mary, was born at Flete. In November of the same year I was able to greet my parents on the platform of Plymouth station. They had joined us from Palestine. Our wartime travels were over.

In the subsequent security and quiet of our home in Britain I could look back dispassionately on my life and the war years. Of all places in the world, I knew that only Britain could offer us true freedom and a way of life which, different though it was in detail, would satisfy the longing for the true values in life felt by any man or woman belonging to the Western world. The more I cast my mind back over the years the more distinctly I could see the hand of God guiding me unerringly through all the years of toil and tribulation. I began to pity the humanist and the atheist who must always talk about coincidence whenever something unusual and unexpected happens.

Too many 'coincidences' took place in my life for them to be merely coincidences. I had diphtheria and survived. I had cholera and survived. I had typhus and survived. I had malaria and survived. I survived a motorcycle accident which left me lame: except for my mother, everyone had given me up for dead. I was machine-gunned at close range several times, even

196

as a child. In 1939 I escaped shooting by the Russians owing to the unexpected intervention of a commissar. And lately there was our escape to the West: the choice of Cieszyn instead of Bohumin to cross the border; the meeting with Mr Smotrycki at Cieszyn and the subsequent opening of the Czechoslovakian border: the meeting with the Bundas on the train; the registering at the police station in Prague on Saturday noon, so avoiding the necessity of registration with the Security Police; the help of the Czechoslovakian Border Guards; the timely change of the American Border Guard; the attitude of the C.I.C. major at Furst-am-Wald; the appearance of John at Furst; the boarding of the train at Furst; the attitude of Captain Hanson; Irena's meeting my mother's friend at Innsbruck, who took her and her children over the Italian border. Twenty or more 'coincidences'. Surely when they come in such numbers coincidences stop being 'coincidences' and have to be called Providence.

XXI

Epilogue

THIRTY-FIVE YEARS had gone by since our Plymouth days when, on our annual holiday in Sweden, we heard on the BBC World Service and on Warsaw Radio about the events in Gdansk which led to the birth of the Free Polish Trade Union, Solidarity, and later to the introduction of Martial Law in that country.

Suddenly Poland was news again: innumerable articles, interviews with politicians, and clever analyses appeared in the Press and on other media.

In view of my first-hand experience with Soviet methods, I feel that I am qualified to add a few words about the situation in Poland as it is now. I venture to do so as a fitting finale to my reminiscences.

In 1945 Poland, albeit unwillingly, became a satellite of the USSR. It seems to me that no politician in the West could disagree with this statement. Although totally in Russian power, she was at the same time a boil on the seemingly healthy and unbroken skin enveloping the Soviet Empire. Anti-Soviet and anti-communist partisans were operating in Poland as late as 1947 (so far as I remember); there was the mutiny of 1956, then that of 1970, and that of 1972. In between, Poland seemed quiet, but the Kremlin was never sure of what would happen next.

Developments in Poland in 1981 brought back to my mind memories of events in Soviet Russia between 1921 and 1927.

After the end of the war with Poland and the final destruction of the anti-Bolshevik forces, Soviet Russia seemed to be at peace, within itself and with the world. Stalin knew, however, that many potential enemies of his régime remained untouched. He introduced, therefore, in 1921 his N.E.P., the New Economic Policy. Free trade and independent industries were allowed to operate and flourish again. Normal postal services with Poland and other free countries were reintroduced. Even visits to relatives in Poland were made possible. Poles could visit their relatives in all parts of Soviet Russia. In this way everyone with initiative and drive, who had individuality and some money left, with relatives abroad and contacts with them, came, as it were, to the surface. In 1927 Stalin suddenly abolished the N.E.P. and all who had had anything to do with free enterprise, or had relatives abroad with whom they had been corresponding, disappeared, arrested, shot or deported to the farthest corners of Siberia. 1927 was the last year in which my family had any news about those of my relatives who stayed in Soviet Russia.

Those who were left were the people Stalin wanted in his country: listless, without initiative and individuality, a mass properly conditioned to be obedient and passive. The few dissidents who would appear in the future could easily be dealt with. There are no problems now with the Russian masses and we all know how the authorities deal with people who think differently.

It seems to me that it is very likely that this same method of trying to find a 'final solution' to the Polish problem was decided upon in the Kremlin when the Solidarity movement appeared. The idea was to let them develop, let them bring to the surface all who show initiative, who think as individuals, who can show that they have the will and the ability to lead others.

However, because of what had happened in East Germany in 1953, in Hungary in 1956, in Czechoslovakia in 1968, because of the bloody disturbances in Poland in 1956, 1970 and

199

1972, and finally because of Afghanistan, a pretext had to be found to finish off, once and for all, the independence movement. Informers, stooges and provocateurs were therefore introduced into Solidarity. They must have had orders to incite the members of the movement to make excessive demands, constantly to provoke the Party by staging strikes and takeovers, by remodelling Solidarity into a purely political organ. With true Polish enthusiasm, the nation began to gain a sense of reality, of the hard political facts of life, namely that in no way could or would Soviet Russia allow real freedom to blossom. Freedom is contagious, and to communism freedom is a mortal danger.

Food was gradually withdrawn from the cities, strikes (provoked and unprovoked) brought industry to a standstill, massive foreign debts hung over the nation, a sword of Damocles. The excuse was found and martial law was introduced on 13 December, 1981.

We all know the results. Many thousands of Solidarity members, intellectuals, leaders of all sorts, people who know how to express and justify the discontent on one hand and the expectations of the people on the other, have been 'interned'. The world knows all about the meaning of internment in the communist vocabulary. The régime has achieved the objective set by the Kremlin: try for a 'final solution'.

The 'final solution' must and will fail in Poland. Innumerable Sakharovs and Solzhenitsyns will be always found in Poland and from the toil, from the blood and the ashes, sooner or later freedom in Poland will rise again, a Phoenix come this time to stay.